Measured Drawings
of
Early American Furniture

William Savery High-Boy—1760-1775

Measured Drawings
of
Early American Furniture

$\longleftarrow \bullet \bullet \bullet \longrightarrow$

BURL N. OSBURN

AND

BERNICE B. OSBURN

Dover Publications, Inc., New York

Copyright © 1975 by Dover Publications, Inc.
Published in Canada by General Publishing Company, Ltd., 30 Lesmill Road, Don Mills, Toronto, Ontario.
Published in the United Kingdom by Constable and Company, Ltd., 10 Orange Street, London WC 2.

This Dover edition, first published in 1974, is an unabridged and corrected republication of the work originally published in 1926 by The Bruce Publishing Company, Milwaukee.

9-29-10   15-95

International Standard Book Number: 0-486-23057-0
Library of Congress Catalog Card Number: 74-79936

Manufactured in the United States of America
Dover Publications, Inc.
180 Varick Street
New York, N. Y. 10014

TABLE OF CONTENTS

PREFACE

Age alone is no guarantee of worthiness. Age alone is, perhaps, sufficient reason for the collection of any class of objects, yet collections are justified because no designer is able to create or plan an entirely new article, but must largely depend on collecting and rearranging elements from old material. This dependence makes it more necessary that collectors, whether individuals or institutions, should gather objects of particular merit, and aid in the spread of knowledge of them. Designers are depending more and more on museums, and fortunately, museums and private collectors are taking the helpful attitude.

Exact reproductions are desirable when the object copied combines in itself beauty, utility, and adaptability to modern needs; if one of these is lacking, it should be supplied in the copy. Each person who copies an old object must decide for himself whether the reproduction should be literal, or to what extent it should vary from the original. The permanent value of the reproduction depends on the degree of good judgment and taste used in such selection and variation.

In the field of household equipment, and particularly furniture, this axiom leads us to inquire as to the forms and designs that have been most persistent in use, most enduring in construction, and most satisfying in appearance. Perhaps no one piece can combine within itself the ultimate in all of these requirements; yet it is possible to find those that are unquestionably superior in one or more, and satisfactory in the others, or at least capable of modification. It is with this object in view, that this material was gathered, keeping entirely to the product of our own early American designers and cabinetmakers. Although these men were obliged to turn to the works of the past for their inspiration, as we are, they used such judgment that their works are eagerly sought and copied today.

Not only does much of our early furniture have an artistic value, but, as a real "made in America" product, deserves the interest and study of all Americans. As a vital part of American history, the creators of our early furniture merit much more than a casual treatment in our schools. There is a great deal more value to be obtained from reproducing these pieces than the mere handwork involved. One cannot study them without understanding just a little better the aims and ideals of the men who created them, and developing an appreciation of the customs and lives of the people who used them.

Acknowledgment is made to the individuals, and officials of institutions, whose courtesy and interest have made this work possible. The name of the owner of each piece is included in each of the drawings. Thanks are due each of these for permission to measure, examine, and photograph these pieces. Photographs of museum pieces are by courtesy of the Art Institute, Chicago, Ill.; Essex Institute, Salem, Mass.; Metropolitan Museum of Art, New York City; National Museum, Independence Hall, Philadelphia, Pa.; Rhode Island School of Design, Providence, R. I.; (including plates from the Lockwood Catalog); and the Wayside Inn, Sudbury, Mass., Mr. Henry Ford. The frontispiece and the photographs in the chapter on American Furniture and Its Makers are by courtesy of the Metropolitan Museum of Art.

Sioux City, Iowa   B. N. O.

Note to Reprint Edition: The block-front desk pictured on page 13 is now owned by the Art Institute of Chicago. The Duncan Phyfe dining table with center extension pictured on page 15 is no longer in the collection of the Metropolitan Museum of Art.

EARLY AMERICAN FURNITURE

"A chair of oak,—
Funny old chair, with seat like wedge,
Sharp behind and broad front edge,—
One of the oldest of human things,
Turned all over with knobs and rings,—
But heavy, and wide, and deep, and grand,—
Fit for the worthies of the land,—
Chief Justice Sewall a cause to try in,
Or Cotton Mather to sit—and lie,—in."
Parson Turell's Legacy,
Oliver Wendell Holmes

AMERICAN FURNITURE AND ITS MAKERS

According to the plan and arrangement of the American Wing of the Metropolitan Museum of Art, the history of American furniture is divided into three periods. The first period, of late Gothic tradition, is approximately between the years of 1630 and 1725; the second period, showing the influence of the Renaissance, from 1725 to 1790; and the third period, characterized by the classical revival, from 1790 to 1825.

The division of American furniture into these groups, however, can only be approximate, because, due to the wide differences in locality, economic conditions, and traditions of the colonies, styles appeared at different times in each, and held sway with various degrees of persistence.

American furniture, up to the Empire period, followed very closely the current styles in England. This was only natural, for the first cabinetmakers of the colonies were, no doubt, of English birth and training. The spirit of the original styles was carefully preserved, though there were variations in detail due to lack of tools or materials, local influences, or the individuality of the cabinetmaker himself. Because this furniture was the work largely of independent cabinetmakers, these variations were not consistent enough to produce a distinct style, but there were a few instances, such as the block-front desks by Goddard of Rhode Island, and the furniture of Duncan Phyfe, that had no counterpart in England.

Very little furniture of home manufacture was found in the southern colonies of Virginia, Maryland, and the Carolinas. The wealth of the planters made it possible for them to order furniture "in the newest fashion" from England, or from Philadelphia. That which was out of style was given to servants, or often burned. In the central colonies and in New England, the settlers found it necessary, because of lack of means, to use home-made furniture; then, when more prosperous times came, native thrift relegated the old pieces to the attic, instead of entirely discarding them. These pieces, with the old inventories, sale notices, letters, advertisements, etc., constitute the sources of the information we have concerning the early cabinetmakers and their work.

Spindle-Back Chair—Late Sixteenth Century

Wainscot Chair—American—1623

This early furniture, in the Elizabethan and Jacobean styles, was stout even to clumsiness, severe in form and line, and simple in construction. The English originals were made of oak, or occasionally ash; but as pine was plentiful in New England, and possessed the property of being easily worked, it was often substituted. Other native woods used were ash, elm, maple, cherry, birch, walnut, and oak.

The chest was an important piece of colonial furniture, so that pine chests are among the most plentiful of early pieces. They served as seats, trunks, and storage space. The earliest ones were simply boxes with lifting tops. By the middle of the seventeenth century, a drawer was added at the bottom, and a till or tray inside the chest itself. Still later, the one drawer was supplemented with two or three more, so that by the eighteenth century they were not chests *with* drawers, but chests *of* drawers —the forerunner of the chest-on-chest, and the modern bureau.

The high-backed settle and the "joyned" stools completed the seat-

ing capacities of the earliest homes. The settle was built in near the fire-
place, so that it cannot be classed exactly as mobilary furniture. There
were but few chairs of the Jacobean styles made in America. The wainscot chairs were too heavy, and the carved Flemish chair was too elaborate
for the cabinetmakers to attempt often.[1] The Carver and Brewster
chairs, that were possibly brought in the Mayflower were better models
for them. These had turned legs, continuous with the back which was
filled in with a row of spindles. Later in the century, the bannister-back
chair came into use as a native substitute for the beautifully carved
Flemish chair. The bannisters in the back took the place of cane, which

Carver Chairs—Ash and Maple—American—1650-1700

was difficult to obtain. The bannister-back, shown in this collection, has
the arched top rail similar to the original type. This places it as a transition piece, since the later ones had straight top rails. It was during this
time that the very popular gate-leg table was introduced. Two of these
are shown in the drawings; the trestle-foot and the tilt-top tables, the
latter also known as a "tuckaway" table. These have the excellent vase-
shaped turnings characteristic of the Jacobean style. Similar to these are
the tavern tables that were much used at the time. These were small
and light enough to be grouped together for greater sociability during
games, or while drinking. The examples shown here have the Jacobean
characteristics of vase-turned legs, and heavy stretchers placed near the
floor. It was customary to pick these tables up and carry them to the cus-
tomer wherever he sat down.

The ascent of William of Orange to the throne of England marks
the introduction of the William-and-Mary style. Walnut was such a
favorite wood for this furniture, that this date is usually termed the beginning of the "age of walnut." It was used as solid wood, or as a veneer
over oak or soft woods. Oak was still used, particularly at the beginning
of the period, but in America, where the finest walnut could be obtained,

---

[1]Nutting considers it very improbable.

the latter was the favorite. The distinguishing characteristics of William-and-Mary furniture are the ogeed and flat arched aprons, the
straight cup-turned legs, and the curved stretchers. These features are
all illustrated in the walnut high-boy. This is a typical piece of the plainer
type of furniture, in which the craftsman relied on the simplicity of
design and the beauty of the veneer, rather than on ornamentation. Many
such pieces were made in New York, West Jersey, and Pennsylvania,
where high-boys, low-boys, tables, and stools were patterned after English styles. The gateleg table was still popular, as well as a variation of it
in the "butterfly" table. Writing furniture, desks, and tables were made
with slant, or flat tops, turned legs, and shaped stretchers like those of the
high-boy. Bedsteads became more numerous during this period because
of the greater prosperity of the colonists, though it is doubtful whether
any but the simplest were made here. These were of the four-poster type,
with the tester, or canopy, and hangings supported by carved, round, or
octagonal posts. The day bed and truckle, or trundle bed, served for the
younger members of the family, or for servants. The day bed in this collection was probably of this time, though it shows characteristics of an
earlier period.

It must be remembered that styles in the colonies lagged from a
decade to a generation behind those of England, particularly in the earlier
days. After 1700, the colonists had closer communication with England,
with the result that styles appeared here much sooner after their origin
there, than before this time. Very often, travelers or ship captains were
given commissions to purchase furniture for a certain purpose, with the
one stipulation that it be "in the latest style." Here, more than in England, the periods during which certain styles flourished overlapped, and
the transition from one style to another was less rapid. Favorite styles persisted long, especially in outlying communities. Despite this, the Queen
Ann style, introduced into England about 1702, soon became very popular
in the colonies. It was more elegant than the Jacobean, and found favor
with the colonists whose prosperity had created a demand for better homes
and finer furniture.

This style marked a distinct change in furniture construction—an
increasing tendency toward the lighter and more graceful lines. This
tendency persisted throughout the Queen Ann and the early Georgian
periods. The straight, turned legs and the plain structural lines were dis-
placed by the cabriole leg, and the curvilinear element in the chair seats
and backs, bureau fronts and pediments, and legs of tables and chairs.
The stretcher was used with this cabriole leg in the early part of the
period, but was soon abolished to achieve a lighter and more graceful
effect. Mahogany was introduced, and soon became popular. It was
used here before 1720, for records dated before that time have been found
to mention it. More of the furniture used by the colonists was made here
than before this period. The high-boy had become a very popular piece of
furniture, and remained so in the colonies where it reached a much higher

development than in England. Tops became higher in the pediment form, while the base was very similar to the low-boy shown in this collection.

Chippendale became the master cabinetmaker and designer of the later part of this period in England. While it cannot be said that he invented a style of his own, he based his work on the forms in use, and applied to them the prevailing Gothic, Chinese, or French motifs. In his earlier work, the Queen Ann characteristics predominate, but the effects of the classical movement are seen in the straight line construction of his

Block-Front Desk—Made for Brig.-General Ebenezer Huntington, Norwich, Conn.—1800

later pieces. Furniture of both types was made here, as his designs were most enduring, lasting even into the nineteenth century. His influence in the colonies was exerted through his "Gentleman's and Cabinetmaker's Directory," and many close copies of his designs were made by the local cabinetmakers. Some few of his followers so modified his designs as to leave the stamp of their own individuality on them, while in spirit they are still Chippendale. John Goddard of Rhode Island originated the block-front desk — a piece of furniture unknown in England, but very popular in the colonies. The desk shown on this page is an excellent example, showing the moulded feet, and peculiar construction of the drawer fronts that gave the name. William Savery, of Philadelphia, another colonial disciple of Chippendale, is discussed in the following chapter. Although Chippendale designed many kinds of furniture, his chairs stand out as his masterpieces. They are based chiefly on the Queen Ann splat-back chair, but vary greatly by pierced or carved designs on the splat, making it very decorative. The best known designs are the ribbon-back, ladder-back, and fretted backs of Chinese and Gothic inspiration.

In the Georgian period proper, 1760-90, the trend in furniture styles was toward the classical. The Brothers Adam are directly responsible for this radical change in furniture styles, although they themselves were not cabinetmakers, but architects and designers. About the time they became prominent, Pompeii was unearthed, with an effect similar to that of the "King Tut" revival of the past few years, although of a much more permanent and widespread degree. Robert Adam did much to make the classical designs practical, by measured drawings made from the findings of his explorations. The curvilinear element in furniture design, introduced during William-and-Mary's reign, had been paramount until the advent of the Adams, and it is doubtful whether a lesser influence than theirs could have changed it. The whole contour of the furniture was changed; the cabriole leg gave way to straight reeded or turned legs; the claw and ball foot was exchanged for the simple spade foot; and elaborate carving was dropped for egg-and-dart and other classical mouldings.

Since the Adam brothers were designers only, their furniture orders were filled by cabinetmakers who had to be able to modify these designs to make them practical. It was but a step more for these cabinetmakers to use elements of these designs for their own work. Thus Hepplewhite, Sheraton, and many of the minor designers and cabinetmakers received much of the basis for their own work, though each displayed his own originality in their interpretation. Hepplewhite, the earlier of the two, copied the Adams' ideal of ornament rather than the form. The main structural lines of his work are rectilinear, but with many curved lines in chair backs, seat frames, sofas, and settees. Chair and table legs of Hepplewhite's design were usually square and tapered. Hepplewhite's designs were very popular in the colonies, for they were of a type suited to the Georgian houses being built here.

The sideboard, in its present form, was introduced at this time by one of the lesser known designers named Shearer. Hepplewhite copied it, using the serpentine front to give added grace and beauty. Hepplewhite writing furniture consisted of writing tables and secretaries; the former with flat tops, and tiers of drawers on either side of the knee space; the latter a combination of cabinet and drop lid desk. Tables by Hepplewhite were as varied as his chairs; semi-circular tables, in pairs, used to lengthen a rectangular dining table; card tables, work tables, etc. The latter were similar to the several small tables in the drawings. These might be either Sheraton or Hepplewhite, as they have details common to both, but no distinguishing marks. Hepplewhite's book, "The Cabinetmaker's and Upholsterer's Guide," appeared in 1789, with additions and revisions covering about five years more. Since this is but a few years before the "Cabinetmaker's and Upholsterer's Drawing Book" by Thomas Sheraton appeared, it is not unnatural to find a similarity in their designs, a similarity that shows in grace, lightness, and simplicity. Sheraton's preference for straight lines is emphasized in all his furniture. The legs of his tables and chairs were extremely slender, and the round reeded and tapered legs added to the effect of height. His excellent sense of proportion imparted to his furniture a sense of dignity, despite its delicate construction. Many of his tables were very similar to those of Hepplewhite. He had an abundance of small writing tables, card and tea tables.

The additional distinguishing features were round reeded legs, reeding around the edges of table tops, little carving, delicate inlay, and a use of figured veneer for decorative effects.

In the United States, during the last decade of the eighteenth, and the first of the nineteenth centuries, the designs of the Adams, Hepplewhite, and Sheraton, were widely used by the native cabinetmakers, who so blended the characteristic details of each designer that it is difficult to designate any piece as being purely one or another. The furniture made by these cabinetmakers ranged from the very simplest pieces for the hum-

Duncan Phyfe Dining Table with Center Extension

bler homes, to the highly decorated pieces intended for the beautiful Georgian homes that were built during this period. Among this furniture are found chairs, with shield-shaped or square backs; reeded, inlaid, and veneered tables, for every conceivable use; and desks, and chests of drawers, of mahogany inlaid with lighter woods. There were sofas, armchairs, and settees, upholstered in imported fabrics; high post bed-steads, and dressing tables; footstools, and fire-screens; everything needed for the homes of a people who were rapidly becoming as prosperous and luxury-loving as those of the old world.

During the later part of this period, the influence of the Empire style was felt. This style had its origin in France, which at that time was under Napoleonic rule. Napoleon felt the political need of a new style, and induced the French designers to redesign furniture, buildings, dress, etc. The result was a style artificial in detail and motif. At first it was classical; later, Egyptian details were introduced. England followed French lead, and the result was as bad, if not worse. In America, the popular sympathy had been with France for some time, so the Empire style had full sway, both in furniture and dress. The earliest forms retained enough of the elements of the Georgian style to be very satisfactory, but by 1825 they were as heavy, clumsy, and as full of meaningless curves as those of England. This was followed by the Victorian "reign of horror" which is better passed over quickly.

Since the Empire, we have had no distinctive style in furniture, though it is probably the secret hope of many designers that they may one day develop the next American style. If such an event comes, it is reasonable to expect that the style will be based on those forms that have been most truly distinctive in American ideals and traditions.

WILLIAM SAVERY

Lockwood, in his "Colonial Furniture in America," says, "It is surprising to many to find that beautiful pieces such as these * * could have been made in this country. They were certainly the work of cabinetmakers of the first rank, and not only are such pieces found, but chests-on-chests, and tables with pie-crust edges of the same quality are to be found, all traceable to Philadelphia. Who the cabinetmaker was, or whether there was more than one, is not known, but a dressing table of this type has been found in which is pasted an advertisement of the maker, which reads as follows: 'William Savery, at the Sign of the Chair, near the market on Second Street.' He, at least was one of these cabinetmakers."

William Savery lived and worked during the later half of the eighteenth century, at a time when it was not expected that colonial furniture could compare with that of Europe. Nevertheless, it is difficult to find any contemporaneous English furniture that can surpass his masterpieces. It is not known where he learned his trade, but it is evident that he must have had access to the best furniture designing manuals of the period. These designs were probably Chippendale, for his influence predominates in all Savery pieces, particularly in the pie-crust tables, secretaries, low and high-boys.

The frontispiece, a high-boy of especially fine workmanship, embodies many of Savery's favorite details. The cabriole leg with claw and ball foot was used on practically all work. Usually, it was ornamented at the knee with the shell or acanthus motif. The shell with scrolls was also a favorite pattern for the delicate carving common to his pieces. Corners of high and low-boys were finished with a quarter-round carved, or fluted column. A broken pediment, ogeed top, with urn-and-flame finials, completed the high-boys, chests-on-chests, and secretaries. His chairs are similar in outline to those of Chippendale, with the elaborately carved splat-back; likewise his pie-crust tables closely resemble the best of the English master. Practically all of his work is done in walnut and mahogany.

DUNCAN PHYFE

Duncan Phyfe began his trade as a cabinetmaker in Albany, during the last part of the eighteenth century. About 1790, he moved to New York, being attracted by the demand for finer furniture in that city. His shop was located at 194 Fulton Street, where he worked for 52 years. Toward the latter part of his life, his work became very popular among New York's wealthy families, so that he found it necessary to expand his business, until at one time he employed nearly a hundred workmen.

He was unexcelled as a cabinetmaker, though a poor draftsman. The care with which he chose his materials showed that he regarded his work as an art. He used San Domingo mahogany almost exclusively, and none but the finest logs were allowed in his shop; in fact, an especially fine mahogany log came to be known as a "Duncan Phyfe" log, wherever it might be.

Duncan Phyfe Chairs—Medallion Shows Empire Influence

His first work, 1795-1818, was of Adam-Sheraton inspiration, and from the design standpoint was his finest. From 1818 to 1830, the French Empire style was in vogue in the United States, and Phyfe adapted its motifs and spirit in the creation of a distinctive American Empire style. In the first part of the period, he retained enough of the Sheraton influence to keep his work up to the usual standard of excellence; during the latter part the increasing influence of the late Empire forced a deterioration. From 1830 to 1847, he evidently made furniture to suit the popular taste. He, himself, designated it as "butcher furniture."

He excelled in the making of tables—sofa tables, dining tables, card, and work tables. There was little case furniture, though he made a few dressing tables, sideboards, etc.; they were evidently made to fill special orders rather than for general trade.

The Sheraton influence is shown, for example, in the lyre design used as table supports, chair backs, music rack ends, etc. The round, reeded leg of Sheraton design appears in most earlier chairs and tables, and continues to appear in later pieces.

His early American Empire has in it the best elements of both the French and English Empire styles, with the characteristic grace and lightness of the Sheraton style. The table and chair shown here, as well as the table in the drawings, belong to the better part of this period, though the chair medallion is not his best. Most of the decorative details in the carving and brasses are Empire in style; the reeding on the legs and table top edges is a Sheraton detail that persists throughout his work. The acanthus leaf appears in the carving on legs and shafts of tables. The legs usually end in brass paw-shaped, or claw feet. Backs of chairs were commonly rectangular in shape, with various-shaped medallions, lyres, etc., in them.

In the latter half of his work, the furniture loses its graceful sweeping curves, and becomes heavy and clumsy; brasses become too heavy and ornate, so that the only redeeming feature is the beautiful panels of mahogany veneer.

"Phyfe's * * importance in furniture making arises from the fact that he, as the heir of the great cabinetmakers of the end of the eighteenth century, carrying on the tradition of fine design and craftsmanship well into the nineteenth century, presents in his work an example to modern cabinetmakers of the manner in which furniture for contemporary use may be designed in terms of ancient tradition."

—B. B. O.

BIBLIOGRAPHY

*Furniture Masterpieces of Duncan Phyfe, Cornelius.
*Furniture of Our Forefathers, Singleton.
 Furniture Designers of the 18th Century, Simon.
 English Furniture, Robinson.
 Old English Furniture, Percival.
*The Collector's Manual, Moore.
*Colonial Furniture in America, Lockwood.
*The Pendleton Collection, Lockwood.
 History of Furniture, Litchfield.
*Practical Book of Period Furniture, Eberlein and McClure.
*Handbook of Period Styles, Dyer.
 Style in Furniture, Benn.
*The Lure of the Antique, Dyer.
*Furniture of the Olden Time, Morse.
 Present State of Old English Furniture, Symonds.
 Book of Decorative Furniture, Foley.
*Antique Furniture, Burgess.
*Furniture of the Pilgrim Century, Nutting.
*The American Wing, Handbook, R. T. H. Halsey and C. O. Cornelius.

The books marked * have a chapter on American Furniture, or are devoted entirely to the subject.

PENDLETON SIDEBOARD

"In the room downstairs is the sideboard which is very handsome and plain."
—letter to Benj. Franklin from his wife, 1765

This sideboard, in the manner of Hepplewhite, is one of the very fine pieces in the Pendleton collection. The original is of mahogany veneer, inlaid with delicate lines of holly or maple. Examination shows that, if made of solid wood, it would have but few construction features differing from modern practice; principally, in the front and ends which are flush with the legs. Drawers are made, as usual, with dovetailed sides, and with a narrow moulding, or "cockbeading," around the face. This moulding is also used on the two doors. The drawers are inlaid with a single line of holly, placed three-quarters of an inch from the edges, and with quadrant corners. The same plan is followed on the doors, with the addition of a single line near the center opening. All four legs have a double band of inlay around them, near the bottom. On the front pair, this extends in two lines as high as the lower rail, where it meets a band of holly and mahogany. Above the rails are two lines, separated by one-eighth inch of mahogany. The single lines may be made by using the thickness of the holly for the width; the band on the apron may be purchased made up to better advantage than to try to make it.

19

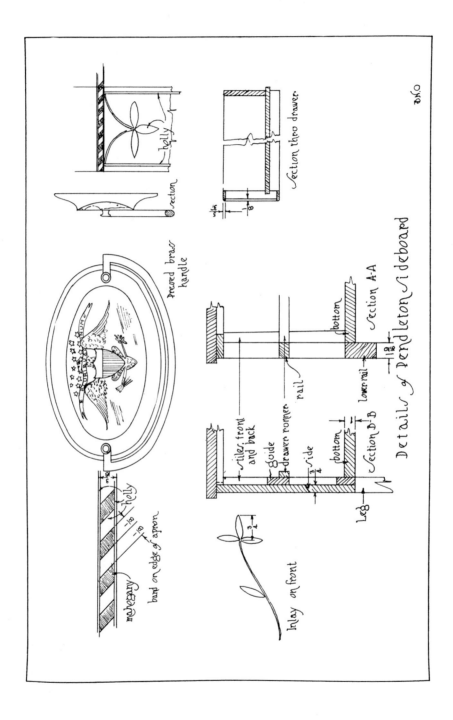

Belly

Section

Pressed brass handle

Section thro drawer

$\frac{5}{4}$

$\frac{1}{8}$

mahogany

Holly

$\frac{1}{16}$

$\frac{1}{8}$

band on edge of apron

Stiles, front and back

guide

drawer runner

rail

side

$\frac{3}{4}$

bottom

bottom

$\frac{10}{16}$

lower rail

Section D-D

Section A-A

Leg

Inlay on front

$\frac{3}{4}$

Details of Pendleton Sideboard

DK0

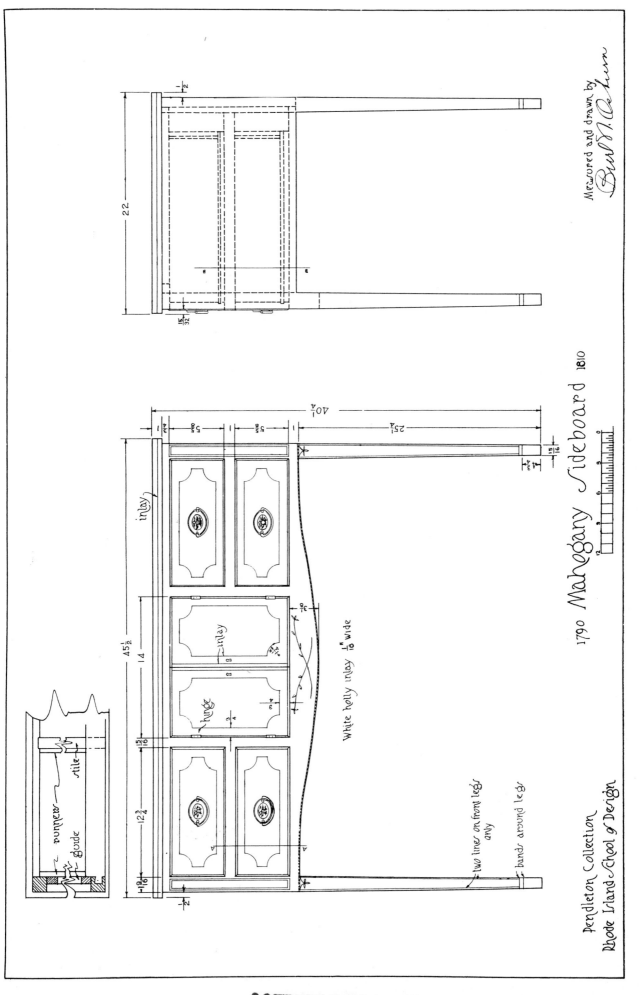

1790 *Mahogany Sideboard* 1810

Measured and drawn by
Burl I. C. Lunn

Pendleton Collection
Rhode Island School of Design

White holly inlay $\frac{1}{16}''$ wide

two lines on front legs only

band around legs

TWO SMALL TABLES

*"Not that 'tis only strong and durable; but ornamental and delightful beyond
expression: What can be more surprising, than to have our chambers overlaid with
Varnish more glossy and reflecting than polisht Marble? No amorous Nymph need
entertain a Dialogue with her Glass, or Narcissus retire to a Fountain, to survey his
charming countenance, when the whole house is one entire Speculum."*

—"A Treatise on Japanning and Varnishing," Stalker and Parker, 1688

These are very simple tables, and are more in accordance with
modern practice in construction than others of the type in this collection.
This applies particularly to the rails and drawer fronts, which are set
back instead of being flush. Drawer construction, with runners, is typical
of modern work. The square-legged table drawer has a narrow front rail
that sets back of the drawer front, under the bottom of the drawer, thus
leaving an unbroken surface on the front of the table. This table is of
mahogany with the sides veneered with curly maple.

*When these pieces were measured, a pair of calipers one-sixteenth
inch thick were used. Consequently, on turned work, in places where two
curves meet to form an acute angle, there will be a slight discrepancy
between the measurement and the true diameter at that point. If calipers
of similar thickness are used, they can be set at the measurement indicated,
and the cutting made to fit them, though the diameter will actually be
slightly smaller. Observance of this will give character and vigor to turnings that would otherwise lack these qualities.*

Two Small Tables

22

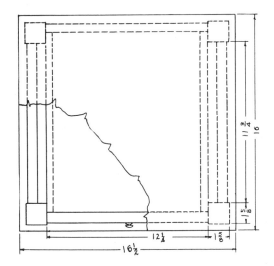

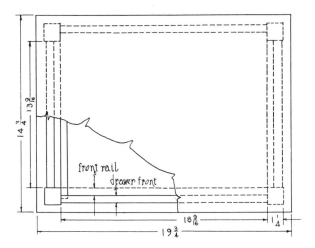

front rail

drawer front

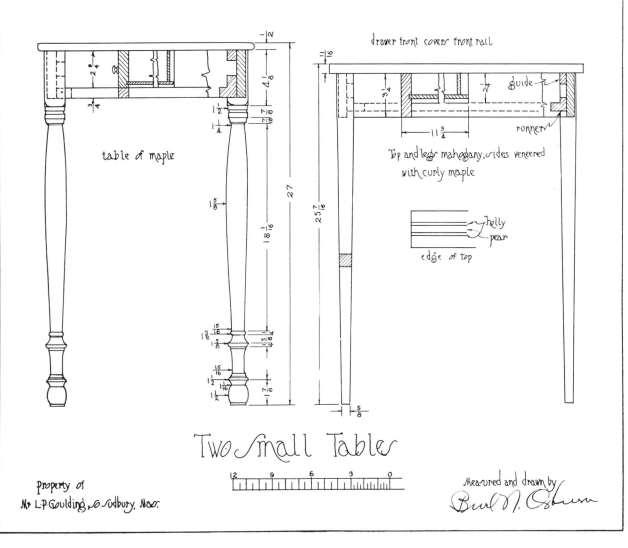

table of maple

drawer front covers front rail

guide

runner

Top and legs mahogany; sides veneered
with curly maple

holly

pear

edge of top

Two Small Tables

Measured and drawn by

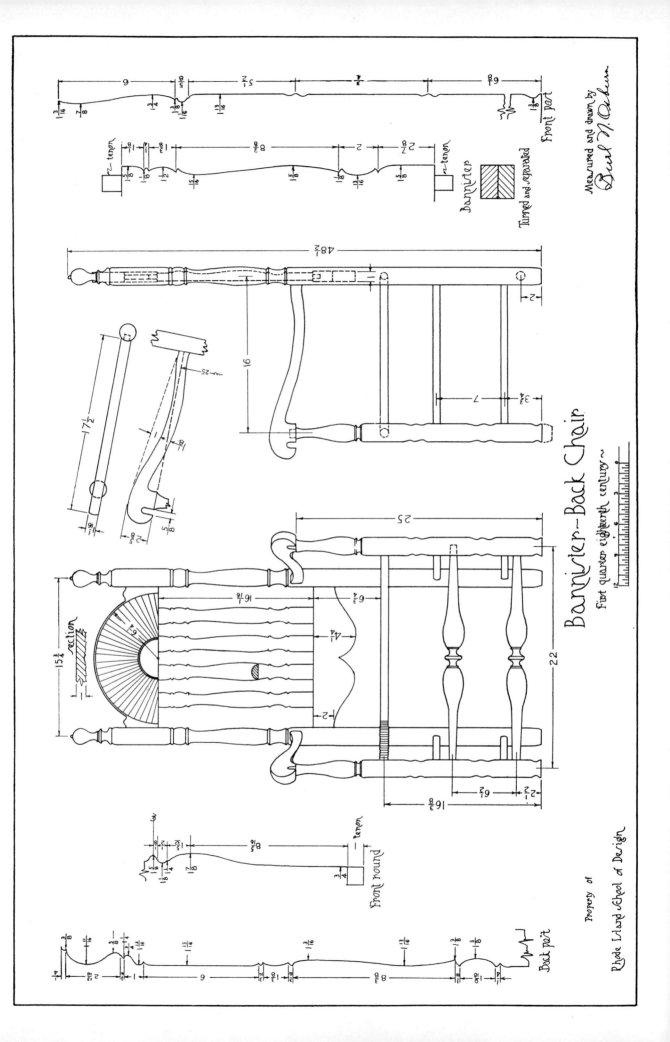

Banister-Back Chair

First quarter eighteenth century ~

Measured and drawn by Paul N. Osborn

Property of

Rhode Island School of Design

BANNISTER-BACK CHAIR

One Ellboe chaire damnified though new, 7s."
— *Inventory, estate of Francis Eppes, 1678*

The bannister-back chair traces its ancestry to the Flemish chair of the time of Charles II. These were elaborate chairs with high, carved backs, cane seats, and turned or "barley sugar" twisted legs. In the hands of the colonial cabinetmaker, with his more limited means, these details were altered to plain turning; the cane and carving disappeared from the backs and were replaced by the ingenious chair-maker first, by leather or upholstery, and later by the split bannister. The cane seat gave way to the rush seat. The original of this drawing is unusual in the four banisters in the back, where three or five are more common, and in the remarkable "sunburst" at the top.

The construction is very simple, as becomes the simple tools and methods of work employed here at the time. All pieces are turned, with the exception of the lower back rail and the two arms. The sunburst, turned as a round disk, is turned to a thickness equal to that at the narrow band around the top, then cut on the diameter, the tenons cut and fit, and the rays cut. These are all flat, with the exception of the concave center one. The bannisters echo the shape of the back posts. They are turned by fastening two pieces, at least ⅞ inch thick and 1⅝ inch wide, face to face, and fastening at the ends, or gluing with a piece of paper between them. After turning, they are separated, and tenons cut on the ends.

The wood of this chair is maple that has, with time, developed a soft brown color from the oil and wax used in its care.

MAHOGANY MIRROR

*" * * when any gentleman is so vain and ambitious as to order the furnishings of his house in a style superior to his fortune and rank, it will be prudent in an upholsterer, by some gentle hints, to direct his choice to a more moderate plan."*
—*"Cabinet Dictionary," Thomas Sheraton, 1803*

"Looking glasses, the most fashionable and elegant," are very commonly found among inventories of household goods of all periods. The mirror shown here is a fine example of the type common to this country during the middle and later quarters of the eighteenth century. The style of this mirror, as that of the smaller walnut one, is very similar to the patterns of one John Elliott of Philadelphia, whose work it might possibly be.

The frame proper is mitered at the corners, while the graceful scrolls are attached by dowels and glue, and are strengthened at the back by small square strips of wood, glued to frame and ornament. The eagle may be made by gluing on a block for the body and head, before the pierced parts are cut out. The wings and tail are cut under the level of the scroll work, as shown by the section. The eagle, the swag, and the concave section of the frame near the glass are gilded, while the remainder is a deep red.

Mahogany Mirror—Eighteenth Century

Note to Reprint Edition: This piece is no longer in the collection of the Metropolitan Museum of Art.

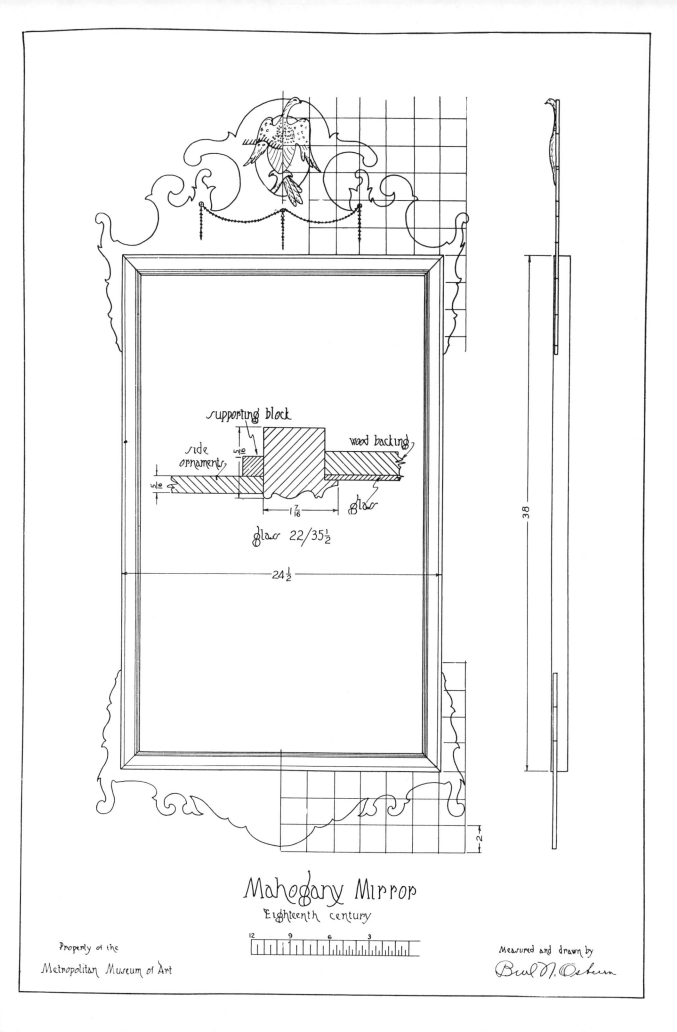

supporting block

side ornaments

wood backing

$\frac{5}{16}$

$\frac{5}{16}$

$1\frac{7}{16}$

glass

glass $22/35\frac{1}{2}$

$24\frac{1}{2}$

38

2

Mahogany Mirror

Eighteenth century

12 9 6 3

Measured and drawn by

Burl N. Osburn

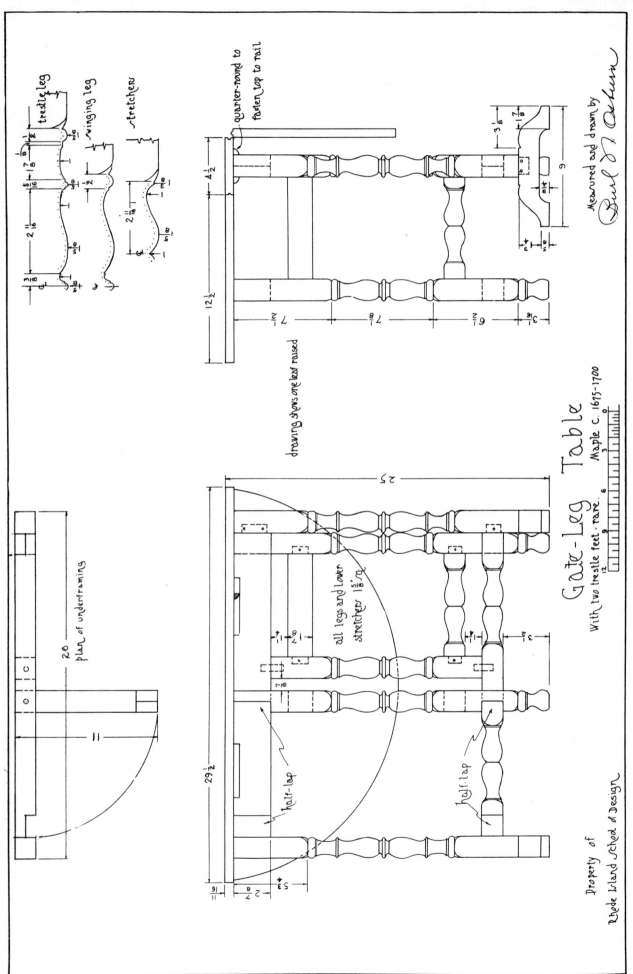

trestle leg

winging leg

stretchers

quarter-round to
fasten top to rail

drawing shows one leaf raised

Measured and drawn by

Burl J. Osburn

plan of underframing

Gate-Leg Table

With two trestle feet - rare.   Maple c. 1675-1700

all legs and lower
stretchers 1⅝" sq

half-lap

half-lap

Property of

Rhode Island School of Design

TRESTLE-FOOTED GATE-LEG TABLE

"For in the country, when we have washed our hands after no foul work, nor handling any unwholesome thing, we need no little forks to make hay with our mouths, to throw meat into them."

—*The Courtier and the Countryman, Nicholas Brown*

This little table was very cleverly planned to make all the turned parts match, so far as possible, when the table was folded up. Its construction is simple when the arrangement of parts is understood. The drawing shows the table in the position shown in the half-tone.

The top is made of two drop leaves, hinged and jointed to a center piece which, in turn, is fastened to the two outer legs and the top rail that connects them. These outer legs rest on trestle feet, and are further connected by a partly turned stretcher near the center of the lower square part of the legs. Two swinging supports are made to open, one on either side of the table, to support the two leaves. Each support consists of four pieces: an outer turned leg reaching from the leaf to the floor; an inner leg reaching from the upper rail to the lower stretcher, and turning on dowels inserted in each; and two connecting rails, the upper one square, the lower one turned. In order that the supports may fold, so as to coincide with the planes of the solid part, the upper rail and stretcher are notched out to half their thickness at the points where the swinging legs meet them. These legs are likewise notched out half their thickness and the width of the rail and stretcher. The top, in the original, is fastened by running dowels through it and cutting them off flush with the surface. All joints are pegged.

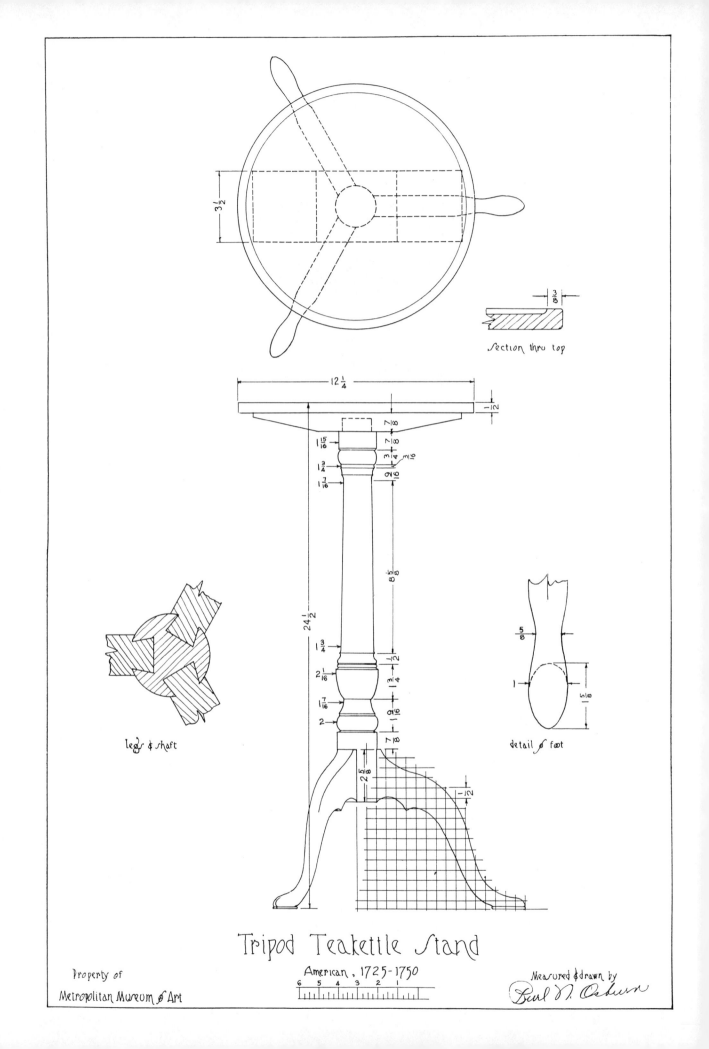

$3\frac{1}{2}$

Section thru top

$\frac{3}{8}$

$12\frac{1}{4}$

$\frac{1}{2}$

$\frac{7}{8}$

$1\frac{15}{16}$

$\frac{7}{8}$

$1\frac{3}{4}$

$\frac{3}{4}$

$\frac{3}{16}$

$1\frac{7}{16}$

$\frac{9}{16}$

$8\frac{5}{8}$

$24\frac{1}{2}$

$1\frac{3}{4}$

$\frac{1}{2}$

$2\frac{1}{16}$

$\frac{3}{4}$

$1\frac{7}{16}$

$\frac{9}{16}$

2

$\frac{7}{8}$

$2\frac{5}{8}$

$\frac{1}{2}$

legs & shaft

detail of foot

$\frac{5}{8}$

1

$1\frac{5}{8}$

Tripod Teakettle Stand

American, 1725-1750

6 5 4 3 2 1

Measured & drawn by

Paul N. Osburn

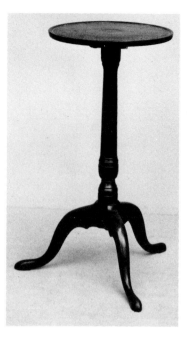

TEAKETTLE STAND

*" * * I got some excellent tea, and I think that I should still be drinking it*
if the ambassador had not charitably warned me, when I had taken the twelfth cup,
that I must put my spoon across my cup whenever I wanted this species of torture
*by hot water to stop * * ."*

—*visitor at house of Robert Morris, 1782*

When the fashionable habit of tea-drinking came into such prominence during the eighteenth century, it developed a complete set of equipment incidental to its technique. The tea-table shown here is made of maple, though other more valuable woods were used. This one is very low, and would serve well today as a plant stand. The design is especially good in the legs. These are gradually narrowed toward the foot, where they widen out again into an oval with a thin "shoe" under it. The legs should be marked out from the co-ordinate diagram, and traced on three pieces of wood previously squared. The grain should run as nearly parallel to the general direction of the legs as possible. A framing square should be set with the tongue under the foot and parallel to it, and the line squared across the top at right angles to the foot. The dovetail should be marked off outside of this mark, and cut before the shaping is started on the leg and foot.

Before removing the shaft from the lathe, mark a circle on it $2\frac{5}{8}$ inches from the lower end, and then cut off the bottom while the work is turning. A paper template, the size of the diameter of the shaft, should be made, and the three dovetails marked out on it from the actual ones already cut on the legs. This is then transferred to the bottom of the shaft, and the lines carried up to the circle. If the cutting is well done, the joint will not require glue. If weakened by any means, a thin metal plate may be fastened to the under side and a screw put into each leg.

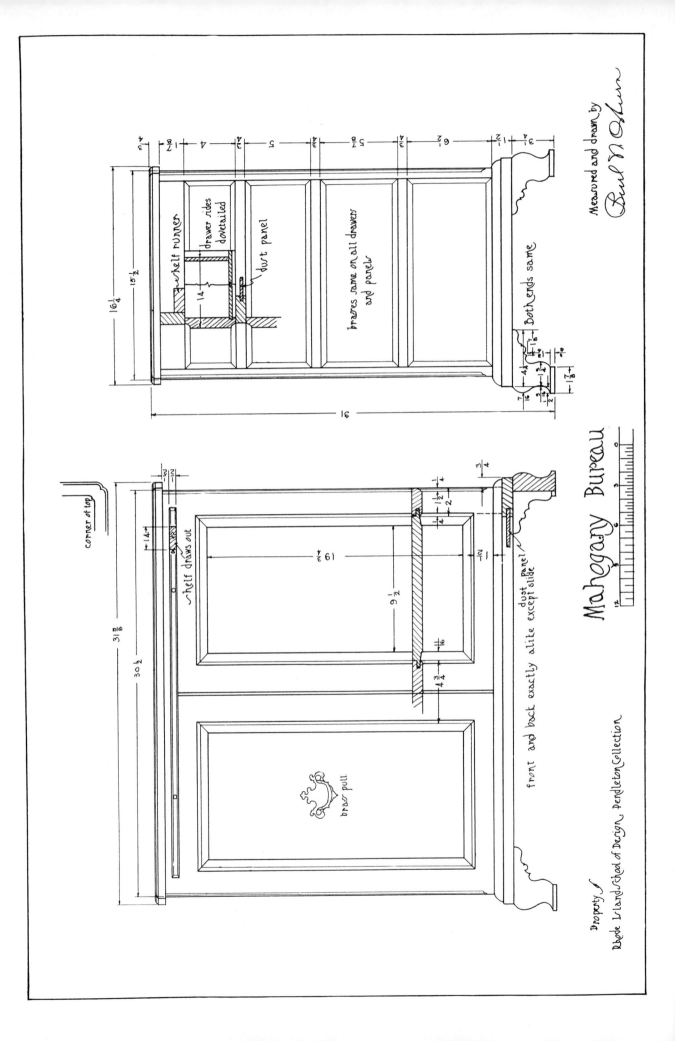

Mahogany Bureau

Measured and drawn by
Burl M Quin

Property of
Rhode Island School of Design, Pendleton Collection

BUREAU-CHEST

*"Gerard Hopkins hath for sale in Gay Street, Baltimore town, mahogany boards
and planks, sawed to suit every branch of cabinet work, as also mahogany logs."*
—*Maryland Gazette, 1773*

This bureau is a peculiar type of chest of drawers, having four drawers of graduated sizes in each end, and a slide, or writing leaf, at the top, which pulls out to one side. The drawers at each end are identical, as are the panels on the sides. The body, or frame, is formed of stiles and rails fitted with panels. The two sides, thus formed, are joined by the drawer rails and runners that are mortised to them. The whole rests on a horizontal frame at the bottom and the juncture, covered with a quarter-round mould. Each drawer runner and rail, and the bottom frame, are grooved out on the inner edge and fitted with a dust panel. The feet are fastened to the lower frame and braced with blocks. The top has a moulded edge and the incised corners common to the time.

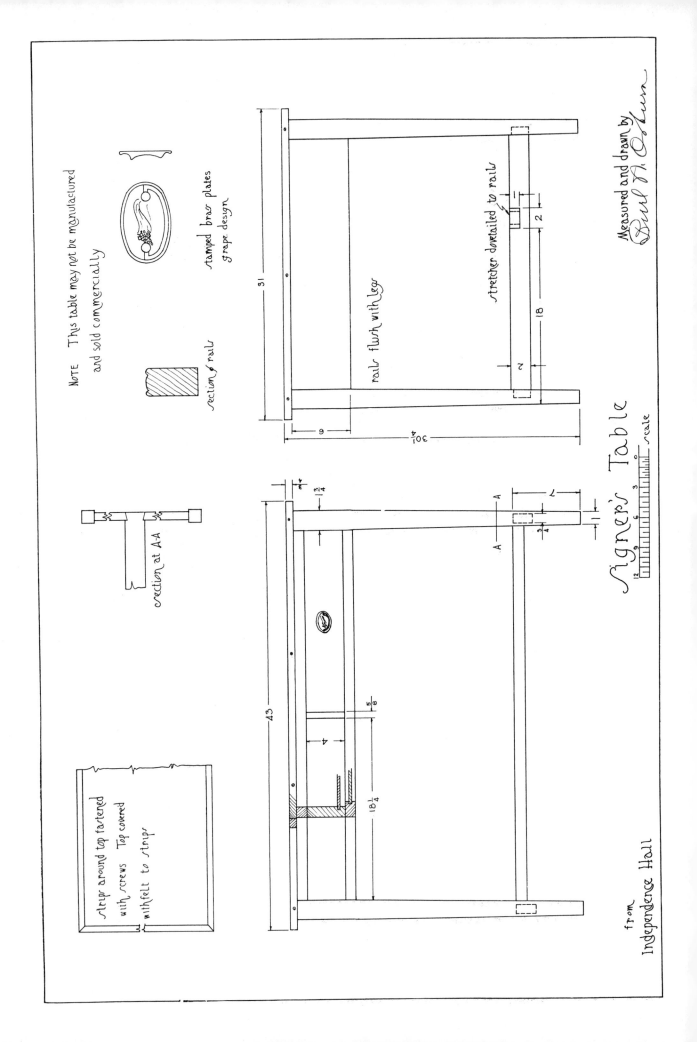

NOTE This table may not be manufactured and sold commercially

stamped brass plates grape design

section of rails

Strip around top fastened with screws. Top covered with felt to strips

section at A-A

31

6

30¼

rails flush with leg

stretcher dovetailed to rails

2

18

2

Measured and drawn by Burl M Osburn

¾
3¼

A

A

2

1

¾

43

5⁄8

4

18¼

Signer's Table

scale
0 3 6 9 12

from
Independence Hall

SIGNER'S TABLE

"I enclose you the bill for your settee and chair which Mr. Fleeson thought it necessary to accompany with an apology on account of its being much higher than he gave Mrs. Shippen reason to expect it to be; he says every material which he has occasion to buy is raised in its price from its scarcity and the prevailing exorbitance of the storekeepers."
—Judge Shippen, Philadelphia, 1775

This table is one of those ordered with the other furnishings of the State House. It is very simple in design and construction. It follows usual table construction with slight variations. The upper rails and drawer fronts are flush with the legs. The top is only slightly larger than the distance across the rails, and is covered with green felt brought down over the edges. A strip, mitered at the corners, is fastened around this to hold the felt in place. The stretcher is set back a comfortable distance from the front of the table, and is visibly dovetailed to the lower rails. These rails are reeded on the upper edge.

A 3/16 inch rounded beading, similar to that used on the Pendleton sideboard, is used around each drawer, and at the lower edge of the upper rails, extending across the legs.

Note to Reprint Edition: The National Park Service of the United States Department of Interior has now proven conclusively that this desk was made in 1790-93 for Congress Hall and has no association with either the Continental Congress or the Pennsylvania State House (Independence Hall).

PINE CHEST

"I would remark, that the cabinet-work executed in this city (New York) is light and elegant—superior, indeed, I am inclined to believe, to English workmanship."
                                    —*Henry Fearon, 1818*

This chest shows an American characteristic in the drawer placed under the box part. No ornamentation is attempted, except the slight chasing on the brasswork. The lid, with cleats at each end, swings on hinges at the back. Inside the box section are cleats across one end and extending about fourteen inches along back and front. These were to support a tray or till. The ends of the chest are gained into the front and back as far down as the drawer top where, on the front, they extend even with the face of the chest. The base is mitered at the corners and fits up around the chest at the front and ends; the juncture is covered with a simple moulding. This is partly cut out in front to permit the drawer to be pulled out.

Brass or iron fittings, suitable for this chest or for any of the pieces shown in this book, may be purchased from a number of dealers. Many of these fittings are handmade, and are splendid reproductions of the original work.

Pine Chest

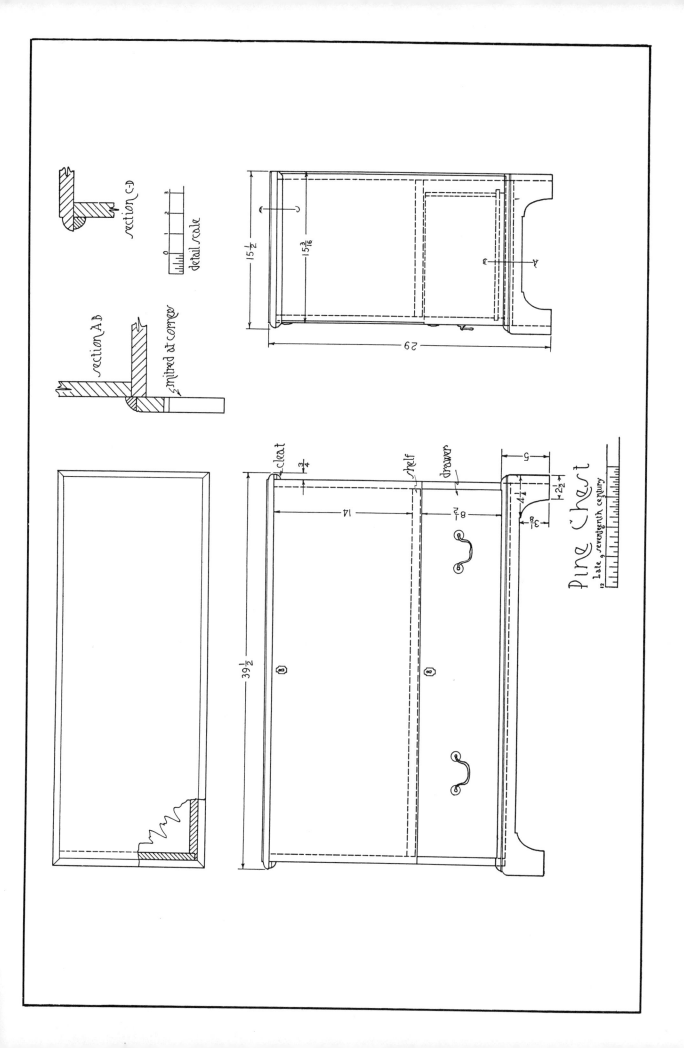

section (C-D)

detail scale
0 1 2 3

15½
15³⁄₁₆

29

section A B

¾mitred at corners

cleat
¾
shelf
drawer
14
8½
5
4¼
2½
3⅜

39½

Pine Chest
late seventeenth century

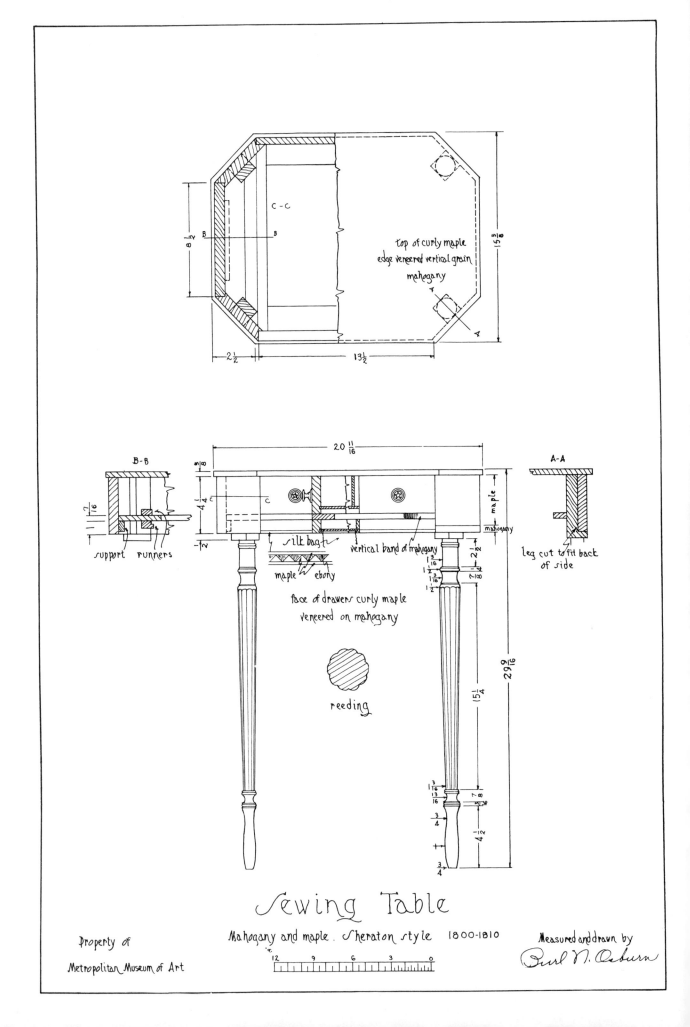

C - C

top of curly maple
edge veneered vertical grain
mahogany

8½

B   B

15⅝

2½   13½

B-B   20 11/16   A-A

maple

mahogany

7/16

4¼   c   c

support   runners

silk bag

vertical band of mahogany

leg cut to fit back
of side

maple   ebony

face of drawers curly maple
veneered on mahogany

reeding

2½

1 3/16
1 3/16
1½

29 9/16

15¼

1 3/16
1 3/16

7/8
7/16

3/4

4½

3/4

Sewing Table

Mahogany and maple. Sheraton style   1800-1810

12   9   6   3   0

Measured and drawn by

Purl M. Osburn

MAHOGANY SEWING TABLE

"In Broad Street, Soho, after a few days' illness of a phrenitis, aged 55, (died)
*Mr. Thomas Sheraton * * * for many years a journeyman cabinetmaker."*
—*Gentleman's Magazine, 1806*

This table is a good example of the American device, mentioned before, of veneering curly maple on mahogany. In this table, the top, part of the sides, and drawer fronts are maple. The edge of the top is veneered with vertical-grained mahogany. A narrow band of the same runs around the sides and across the front drawer rail.

The seven sides are joined and held in place by the top and the frame, of which the drawer rail in front is a part. Blocks at the ends and back hold this in place. Drawer guides for the upper drawer are fastened to the upper side of this frame, while gained runners on the lower side support the drawer or drawer frame. This lower drawer is, strictly speaking, not a drawer, but a bottomless frame on which is hung a deep, pleated, silk bag. The contents are reached by pulling out the lower frame. It is provided with a lock with the key-hole thread escutcheon turned to a horizontal position. The legs are joined to the corner pieces, by having enough of their front cut away to set them flush with the sides.

39

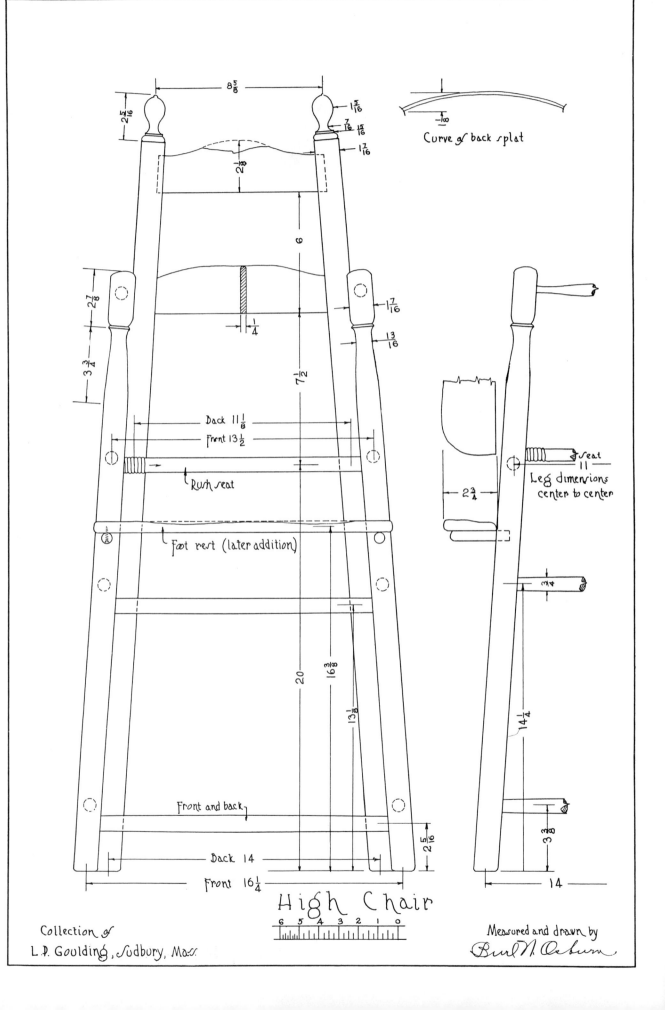

Curve of back splat

Back 11⅛
Front 13½

Rush seat

Foot rest (later addition)

Leg dimensions
center to center
seat
11

Front and back

Back 14
Front 16¼

High Chair

HIGH CHAIR

"On the two tables were fifty large elegant pyramids, with jellies, syllabubs, cakes and sweetmeats. The supper was entirely cold, except several tureens of soup; and consisted of buttered ham, Yorkshire pies, veal, variously prepared, puddings, etc."
—*Gentleman's Magazine, 1778*

This type of chair was common in this country for over a century. It is simple in design and construction, but well planned to prevent tipping. Examination of the original shows the foot rest to be a later addition, though the feet of many generations have worn it almost in two. The rush seat is in a good state of preservation. There is no attached table as in modern chairs. The custom was to put the child directly at the table, though in many families after the elders had finished.

All parts, excepting the back rails and foot rest, are turned. The rounds are slightly crowned in the center. In fitting them to the legs, it will be noted that the side and front (or back) rounds do not enter the legs at the same level, thus preserving strength. The side rounds of the seat are above the front and back rounds, thus making the seat more comfortable. The rounds should not have tenons turned on them, but should be the full diameter of the piece used. If a bit gauge is used, the rounds can be cut to a definite length. The two back splats are very thin, and may be steamed and bent with the tenons left the full thickness of the wood.

41

MAPLE TABLE

"The curled maple is a species of the common red maple, but * * * is very difficult to be got. * * * The wood of the sweet gum-tree is merely employed in joiner's work, such as tables and other furniture, but it must not be brought near the fire, because it warps."   *—1748*

This table reverses the custom of beveling, by applying the bevel to the under side of the top.   The legs are tapered on the inner surfaces only, while the four edges are very slightly rounded.   Sides and back are set flush with the outside of the legs.   All tenons on rails are pegged, as is usual with furniture of the time.

Small Table

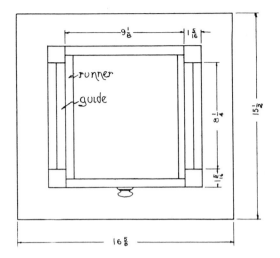

runner

guide

$9\frac{1}{8}$ $1\frac{5}{16}$

$15\frac{1}{2}$

$8\frac{1}{4}$

$1\frac{5}{16}$

$16\frac{5}{8}$

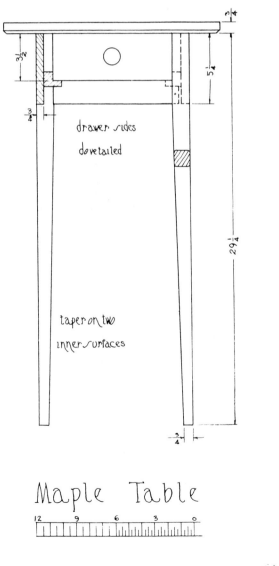

$\frac{3}{4}$

$3\frac{1}{2}$

$5\frac{1}{4}$

$\frac{3}{4}$

drawer sides

dovetailed

$29\frac{1}{4}$

taper on two

inner surfaces

$\frac{3}{4}$

Maple Table

12   9   6   3   0

Measured and drawn by

Burl M Osburn

EIGHTEENTH CENTURY MIRROR

"To be Bought:
* * * A True Looking-Glass of black walnut Frame of the newest Fashion
(if the Fashion be good) as good as can be bought for five or six pounds."
—letter from Judge Sewall, February, 1719

This walnut mirror is similar in construction to the mahogany mirror on page 26. It varies slightly in detail of curves, and in the type of carved ornament on the top. This carved part is cut below the level of the frame, as shown by this section, and is pierced in parts through the wood. The upper corners of the frame are rounded on the front and square on the back. The frame proper is square, but on these two corners it is cut out to a slight depth, and a quarter-round piece, previously turned, is fitted in. The extension side and top piece is cut away to fit over the square part of the frame, leaving only the rounded part visible. A strip of walnut ⅛ inch thick, and as wide as the frame at the outer edge, is glued to it between the side extensions.

On the original, a veneer is applied to the wide ogee curve of the frame moulding in such a way that the grain is at right angles to the length of the frame, and radial at the corners. This is stained a lighter brown than the other parts. The concave part next to the glass is gilded.

Mahogany Mirror—Wayside Inn, So. Sudbury, Mass.

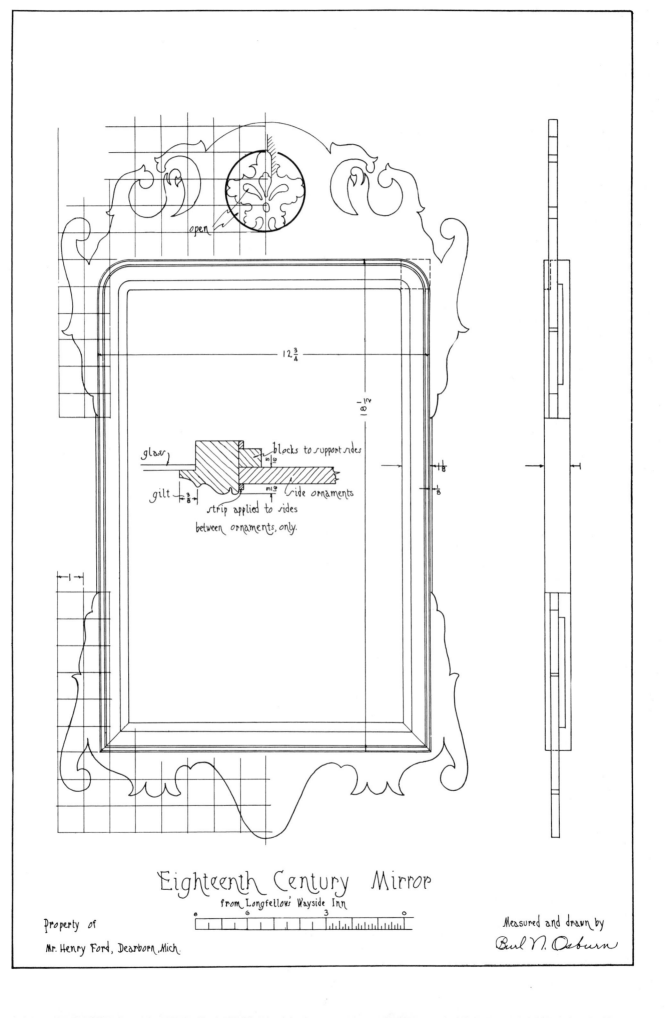

open

12 3/4

18 1/2

glass

blocks to support sides

side ornaments

gilt 3/8

strip applied to sides
between ornaments, only.

1/8

1/8

1

1

Eighteenth Century Mirror
from Longfellow's Wayside Inn

Measured and drawn by

Burl N. Osburn

VASE-BACK CHAIR

"I have one dozen chairs that were made in this country; neat, but too weak for common sitting."   *—Geo. Washington, letter to Richard Washington*

Practically all parts of the chair require lathe work of a simple character. The back legs, which are perfectly straight, may be made in two parts to avoid chattering, though one piece is more desirable. The safest point for division is at the juncture of the straight part with the shaped section, about six inches above the seat. The tenon should be large enough and long enough to give the maximum strength. The side and back rounds are straight with a slight "crown," as in the high chair mentioned before. The front round is very fine and bold. The legs are turned, after building up the feet large enough to give the full-size foot, as shown in the end view. After turning, the back portion is cut away, leaving the "duck" foot.

The seat of the original is of rush, woven over the rounds that connect the legs and the corner blocks at the front. Paper may be substituted for the rush with some advantage.

Vase-Back Chair

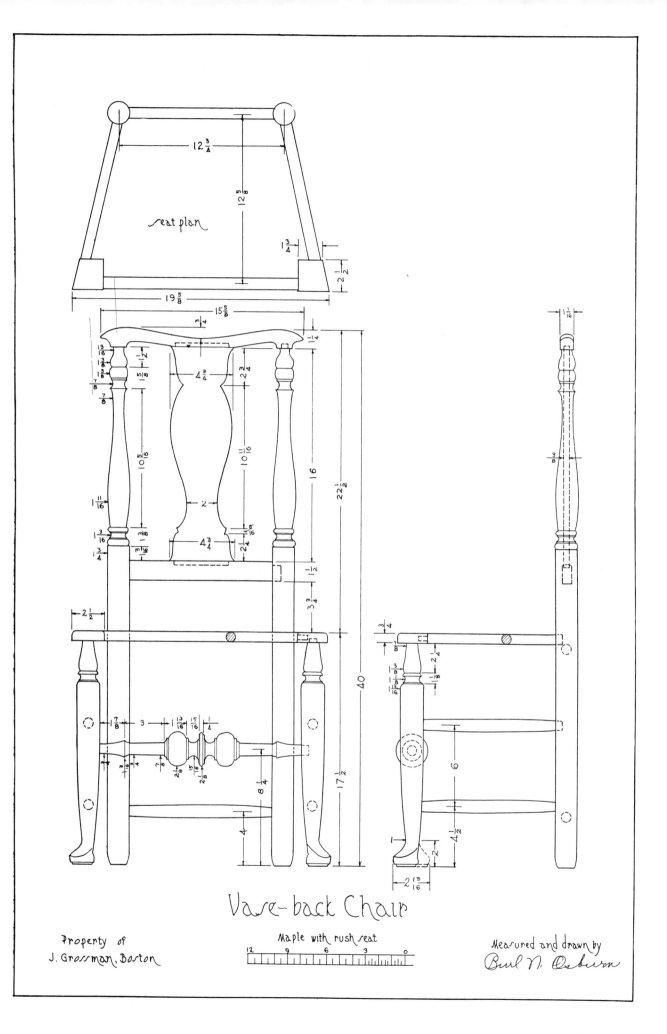

seat plan

Vase-back Chair

Maple with rush seat

Measured and drawn by
Buel N. Osburn

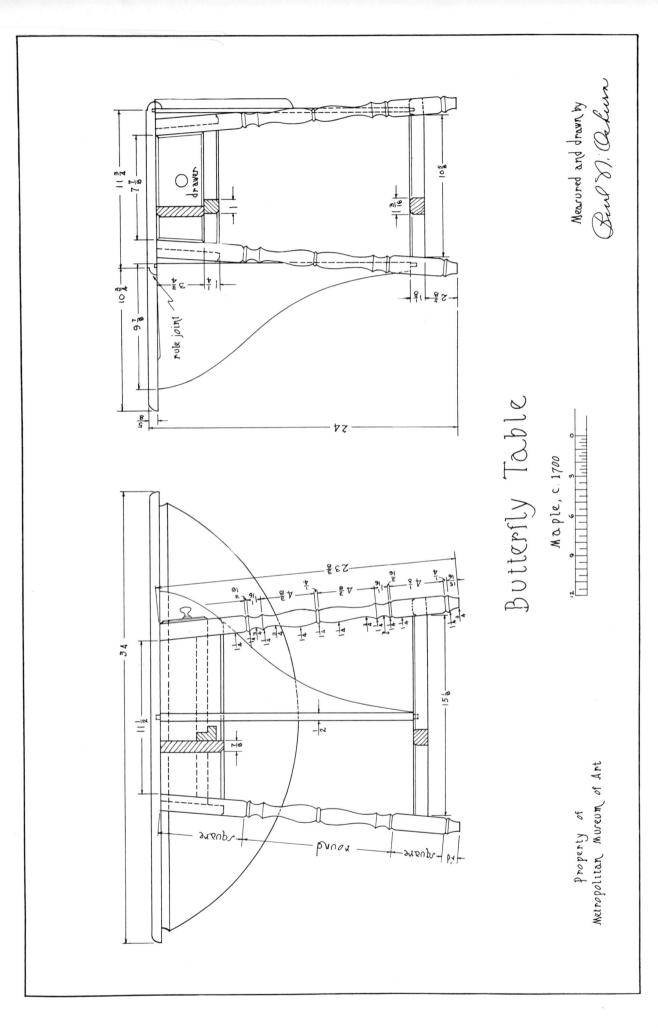

Butterfly Table

Maple, c. 1700

Measured and drawn by

Paul S. Cohen

BUTTERFLY TABLE—MAPLE

"I have been not a little surprised at the extravagance of the Americans in importing mahogany, satinwood, etc., for cabinet work, when they have as good, if not better material at home." —DeWitt Clinton, 1820

This is a later variety of the gate-leg table, and derives its name from the type of support used under the drop leaves. The four legs are connected near the bottom by shaped rails, and at the top by rails shaped on the under edge. The slant of the legs is practically the same from both sides. A drawer with dovetailed sides fits in one end, slides on runners fastened to the side rails, and fits between the front and back legs. The center section of the top is fastened to the four legs with dowels run through the top. The two drop leaves are hinged to this, and work on a rule joint. Holes are bored in the two lower side rails and directly above them in the center section of the top. The wing supports have dowels on bottom and top that turn in these holes. When the supports are folded, the drop leaves hang vertically. The supports are very thin at the edge, particularly at the place where they were handled. The legs are first squared up to the size of the square parts. When turning, the rounded parts on each side of the square sections should be cut first, very slowly and carefully, to prevent chipping off the edges.

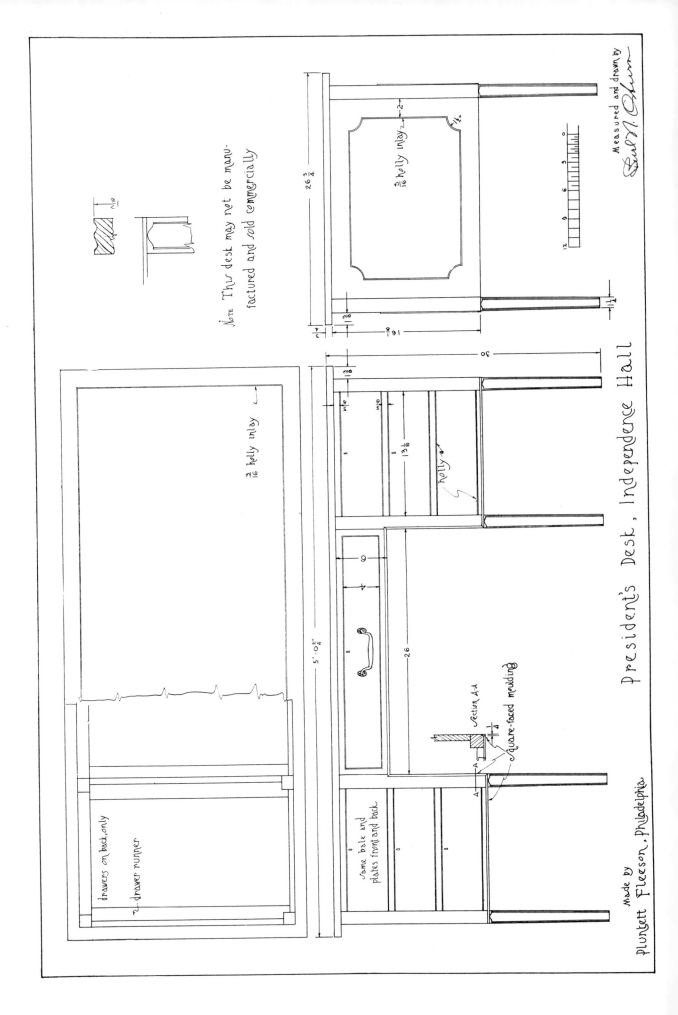

Note This desk may not be manufactured and sold commercially

5/16 holly inlay

3/16 holly inlay

26 3/4

drawers on back only

drawer runner

same hole and plates front and back

square-faced molding

Section A-A

holly

13 7/8

26

5'-0 3/4"

President's Desk, Independence Hall

made by
Plunkett Fleeson, Philadelphia

Measured and drawn by
Earl N. Shum

PRESIDENT'S DESK

*"If these things acquire a superstitious value because of their connection with particular persons, surely a connection with the great charter of our Independence may give a value to what has been associated with that * * * "*
—Thomas Jefferson, letter to his grand-daughter, 1825

During the summer of 1758, when the new State House (Independence Hall) was nearing completion, a committee was appointed by the Assembly to take up the matter of furnishings. Accordingly, Plunket Fleeson was given the order for the desk-table, a tall chair for the use of the assembly president, thirty-two mahogany writing tables, with a like number of arm chairs upholstered with horsehide. Little did this English-born Philadelphia cabinetmaker know of the future in store for the desk he made.

The desk is plain in design, with square, reeded legs. There is a long drawer across the center, and three in each pedestal. A peculiar feature of the desk is shown in its front. Here, the drawer arrangement of the back is imitated exactly, although there are no drawers. The outline of maple or holly is exactly as that on the drawers, where it serves as enrichment and protection for the drawer edges. The drawer pulls are the same. The desk has the original bale, plates, and narrow thread escutcheon on the keyhole of each drawer, both real and false. The top and ends are inlaid with a narrow line. A square moulding, which projects about an eighth of an inch, runs under the lower drawer, up the inner edge of each pedestal, and across the top under the long drawer.

The chair used with this desk is after a Chippendale design. In the top of the high back is the carved sun-burst that led Benjamin Franklin to declare that the sun in that chair "is a rising and not a setting Sun."

Note to Reprint Edition: The National Park Service of the United States Department of Interior has now proven conclusively that this table was made in 1790-93 for Congress Hall and has no association with either the Continental Congress or the Pennsylvania State House (Independence Hall).

TILT-TOP TABLE

*" * * a very handsome stand for a tea-kettle to stand on."*
—letter to Benj. Franklin from his wife, 1765

The construction of this stand is very similar to that of the tea-kettle stand. The feet are fastened in the same way, or by tenons. The mortising may be done on the mortiser by putting the shaft in a half-round cradle and clamping. If the dovetail joint is used and well made, it is not necessary to use glue. The "spade" foot may be cut on three sides on the jointer, and on the band-saw on the inside.

When turning the shaft, a tenon is left on the top to join it to the block that supports the top. Battens are gained into the top, just far enough apart to permit them to pass the block. Dowels are then put through these battens into the block on each side at the front, thus forming a hinge on which the top tips to a vertical position when not in use. When it is dropped into place, a lock, or table catch, prevents it from tipping. The top may be fastened, so that when it is raised, it hangs over one of the legs. This permits the table to be set closer to the wall. The upper edge of the top has a "thumb nail" mould, while the lower edge is beveled to give a lightened appearance.

American Tilt-top Table—
Eighteenth Century

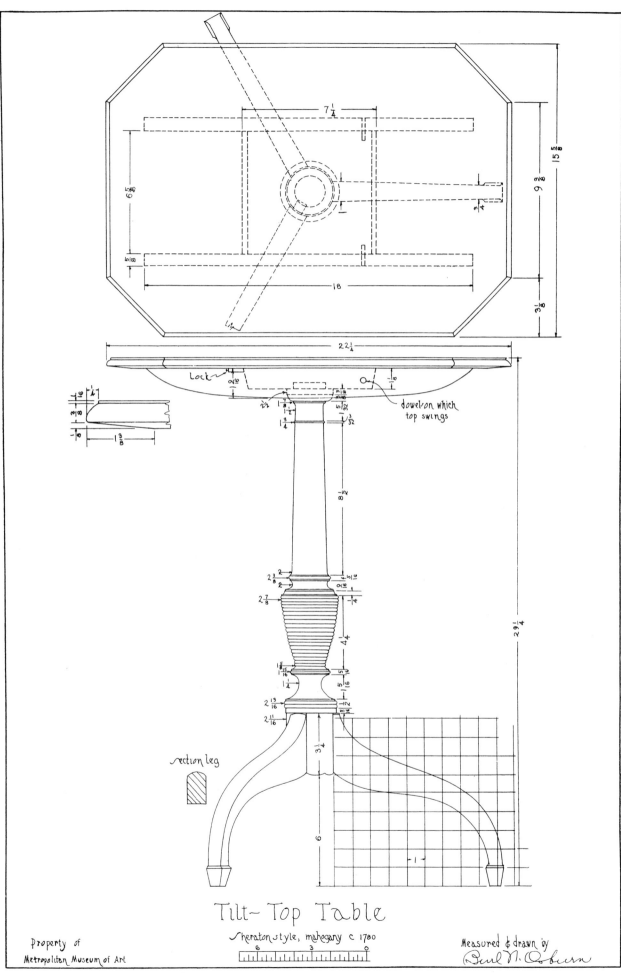

Tilt-Top Table

Sheraton style, mahogany c 1780

Measured & drawn by
Paul N. Coburn

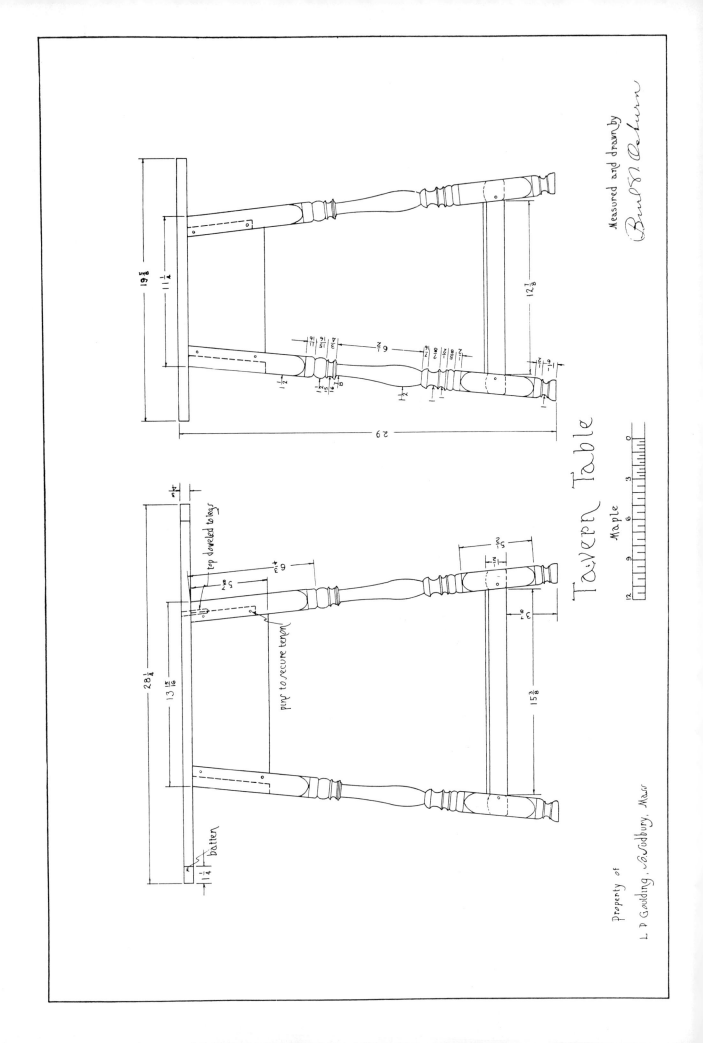

Tavern Table

Maple

Property of

L D Goulding, Sudbury, Mass

Measured and drawn by

Bud S. Coburn

top doweled to legs

ping to secure tenon

batten

TAVERN TABLE

" * * the lord ne the Ladye lyketh not to sitte; now hath eche sych a rule to
eaten by himself in a privee parlour." —Pier's Plowman (14th century)

The drawing does not attempt to show the worn condition of the lower rails where the feet of many travelers have worn away the wood. Tables, stools, and chairs of early periods usually had heavy rails near the floor so that one's feet need not touch the floors, which were made of tamped sand and dirt, stone, or of wide boards with draughty cracks between them.

The rectangular top has battens joined at the ends with tongue and groove joints. The side and end rails are joined to the legs with wide tenons, pinned in two places. In the original, the top is joined to the frame by means of four dowels run through the top into the four legs, and cut off flush. Unless a literal reproduction is desired for some purpose, it is not desirable to do this on a copy. The feet of this table may either have been cut off for casters, or simply worn to their present condition.

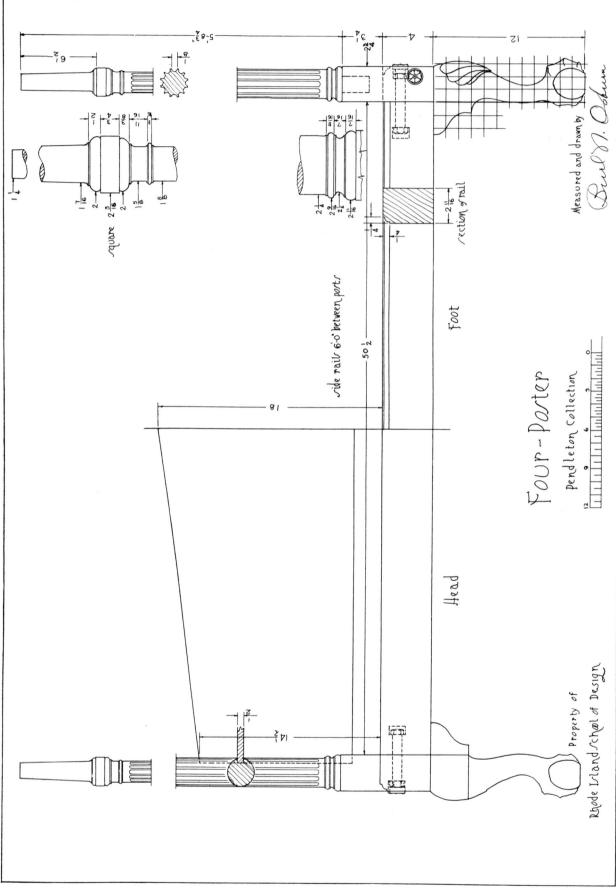

Four-Poster

Pendleton collection

Measured and drawn by
Berel N. Osborn

square

Head

Foot

section of rail

side rails 6'-0" between posts

FOUR-POSTER BED

"Mathew, Mark, Luke and John,
Bless the bed that I lie on."
Old Rhyme

Beds of the seventeenth and eighteenth centuries were made with testers hung about with draperies to protect the sleeper against the winds that came freely through the poorly constructed houses. As buildings became better, the draperies were left off, but the tester or canopy with a short drape remained. The posts may be made in two sections, the lower one ending with the ovolo turning below the fluting. To make this section, the post should be squared up carefully to the size of the square part of the post, and blocks should be glued on two sides to build out for the knee and claw parts. The pattern, taken from the co-ordinate diagram, is marked out on the two adjacent sides that are built up. The piece is then bandsawed, but the scrap pieces are not entirely separated from the posts until all cutting has been finished, because they act as a cradle to support the irregular surface of the leg. After they are removed, the rounding is done with spoke shave, rasp, and scraper. The upper section of the post should have a dowel turned on the lower end. The post is fluted with twelve channels.

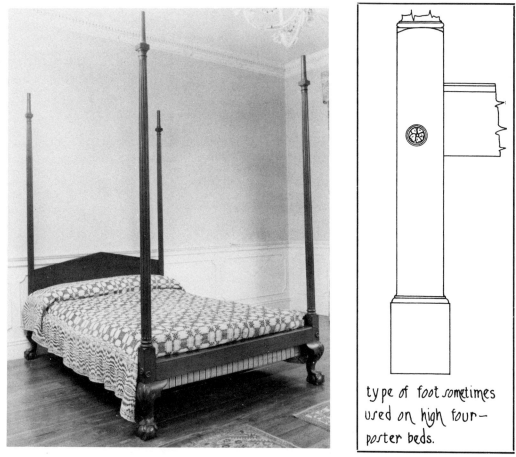

type of foot sometimes used on high four-poster beds.

Four-Poster Bed

It will be found necessary to alter sizes slightly to conform to modern springs. In the original, the four posts separated entirely from the rails and head-piece, but in use were held together by bolts. Holes, large enough for the bolt heads, are bored into the post on two outer sides, at different levels. They are continued through the post with holes the size of the bolt. A hole, at right angles to this, is cut on the inside of the rail to meet the bolt hole. On the outside of the post, a turned rosette is made to insert into the opening. Oftentimes a brass cover was designed to be pivoted just above the opening and dropped down to cover it. The head of the bed is mortised to the two back posts, but not glued, so that it is removable.

OVAL TAVERN TABLE

*"Robert Wallace, joyner, living in Beaver Street at the corner of New Street, makes all sorts of tables, either square, round, oval, or quadrille * * ."*
—*Newspaper advertisement, 1753*

Tables of this type serve the many purposes they did when made, for meals, games, or other uses. They have the advantage of being easily moved about as desired. Construction is obvious from the drawing. The top is fastened to two crossed battens which, in turn, are notched into the side and end rails, and project several inches beyond them. Rails are mortised and "pinned." The top of this table is a restoration.

When casters came into common use, it seems to have been a rather common practice to saw off the legs of old tables or chairs, so that when the casters were put in, the furniture would be at its original height. This may account for the unusually short legs of this table.

Oval Tavern Table

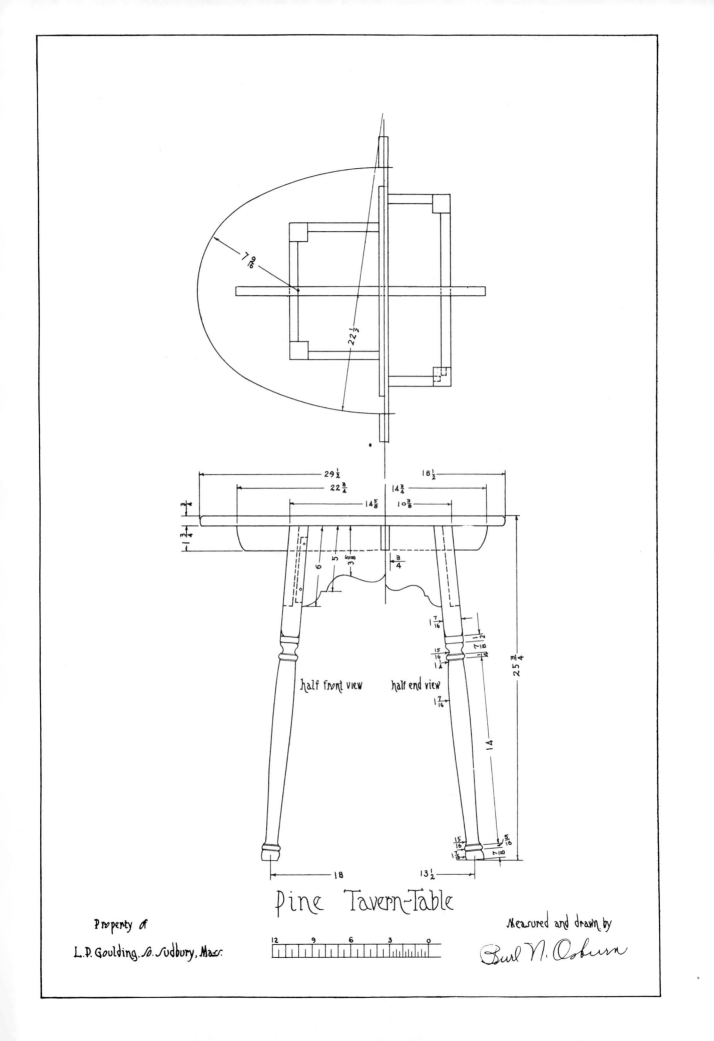

half front view   half end view

Pine Tavern-Table

Measured and drawn by

Burl N. Osburn

DRESSER

"Dined at Mr. Nick Boylston's—an elegant dinner indeed. Went over the house to view his furniture, which alone cost a thousand pounds sterling."
—*John Adams' Diary, 1766*

The dresser is popularly known as a "low-boy." It first appeared about 1690, and came rapidly into favor. It developed in America much faster than England, and was usually more refined in design. It was used as a serving table, and carried the silver and glass-ware, though it was often used, with a movable toilet glass on it, as a dressing table. Examples were made of pine, walnut, cherry, mahogany, and other woods. The construction follows modern practice, except in a few cases. Prominent among these is the visible dovetailing of the rails into the legs, and the stiles into the front apron. The center drawer is carved with a shell ornament centering on a brass knob. It is possible to buy such a carved ornament in composition, so that routing out the space is all that is necessary. The legs are made as described for the four-poster and the wing chair, except that at the knee, the front is left sharp in place of being rounded.

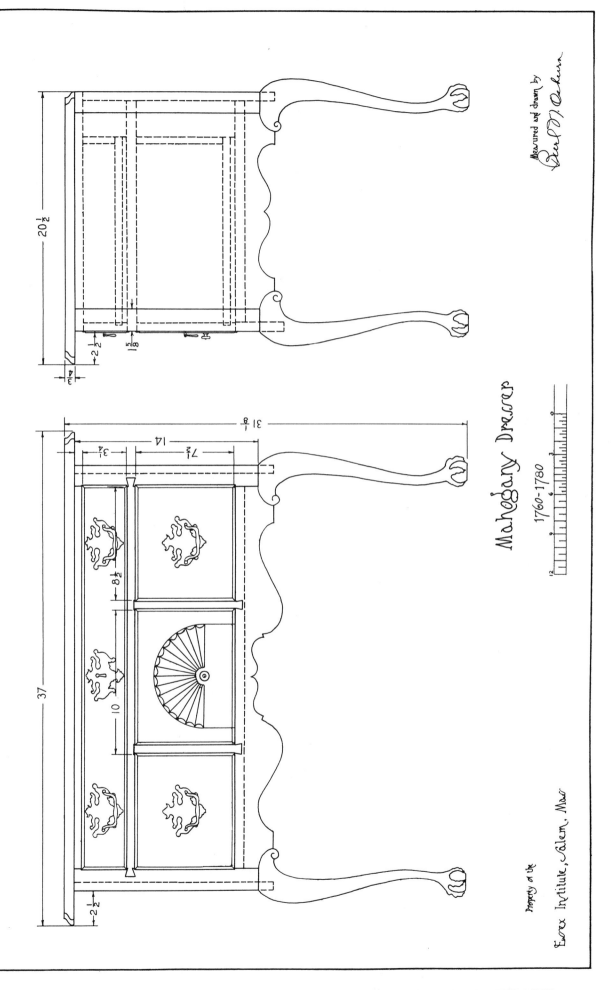

Mahogany Dresser

1760-1780

Property of the

Essex Institute, Salem, Mass

Measured and drawn by

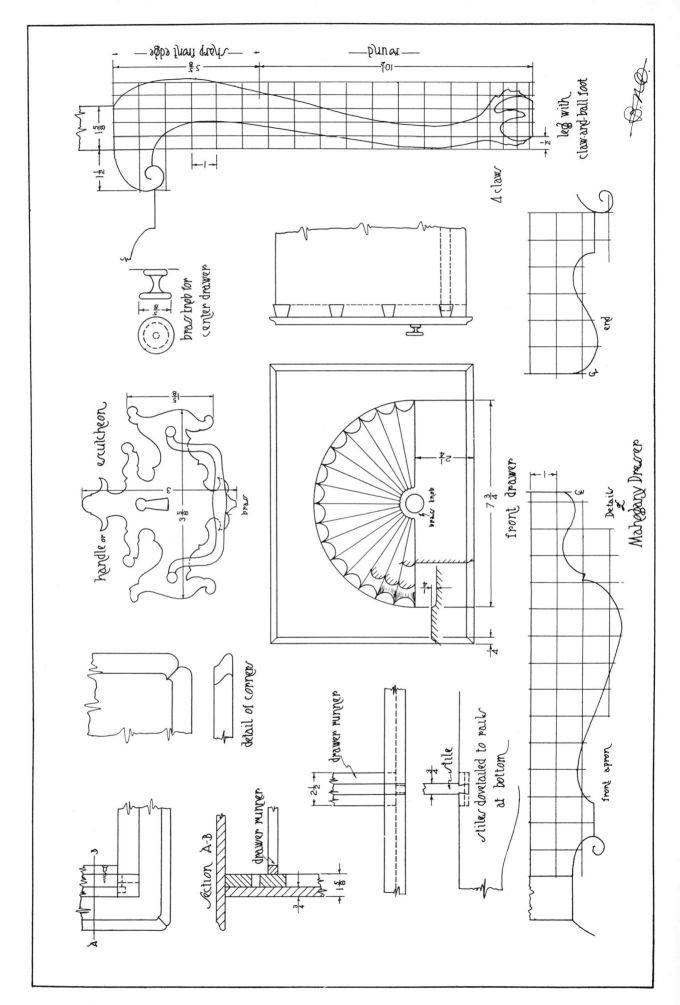

sharp front edge

round

$5\frac{3}{8}$

$10\frac{1}{2}$

$1\frac{5}{8}$

$1\frac{1}{2}$

1

$\frac{1}{2}$

leg with
claw-and-ball foot

4 claws

No. 7

brass knob for
center drawer

$\frac{5}{10}$

handle or
escutcheon

$\frac{5}{10}$

$3\frac{5}{8}$

3

brass

brass knob

$2\frac{1}{4}$

$7\frac{3}{4}$

$\frac{1}{4}$

$\frac{1}{4}$

front drawer

end

3

1

3

Detail
Z

Mahogany Drawer

detail of corner

drawer runner

$2\frac{1}{2}$

drawer runner

$\frac{3}{4}$

Aile

stiles dovetailed to rail
at bottom

Section A-B

drawer runner

$1\frac{5}{8}$

$\frac{3}{4}$

front span

3

A

MINIATURE TALL CLOCK

"James Atkinson, watchmaker from London, appeared and desired to open a shop in the town, which is here granted, he having brought with him upwards of £500 sterling, and being a gentleman of good character."

These miniature clocks are sometimes known as "grandmother" clocks. This one is in perfect proportion, but is only about five feet tall—very practical for the modern house or apartment.

The hood is constructed separately from the body of the clock and slides on at the point indicated. The sides of the hood, from moulding "B" upward, are made in one piece. The front piece above the door is dovetailed to the sides, and the front moulding, including the semi-circular arch over the door, is made separately and mitered to the side moulding B, at the corners over the columns. The thin sides are fastened to the back of B, and at the bottom are gained into C. C is gained out on the under side, to slide on over the section of the moulding fastened to the clock body. The hood door is a half-circle, and fits directly under the moulding B. It hinges to the hood by means of two brass strips fastened at the top and bottom on the outside of the door. A single screw through each of these serves as a pivot; the hinge thus throws the door clear of the column on the hinge side. The moulding of the pediment is band-sawed and then shaped; the top of the hood is thin enough to be steamed and bent in heated cauls, to give the proper shape. The lower third of the shaft, in each column, is turned straight with the entasis beginning at that point, and continuing to the necking. There are eight channels in each shaft.

The body of the clock is of simple construction. It should be built from the top downward. While assembling, temporary bracing strips should be fastened across the back. A thick bottom is sometimes used just above the feet; this aids in giving strength and stiffness. When assembled, a three-eighths inch piece sets into the sides, covering the back. The works are set on a shelf fastened to the body, so that the center of the face is at the center of the open part of the door.

American Miniature Tall Clock
—Thomas Claggett, Newport, 1730-1749

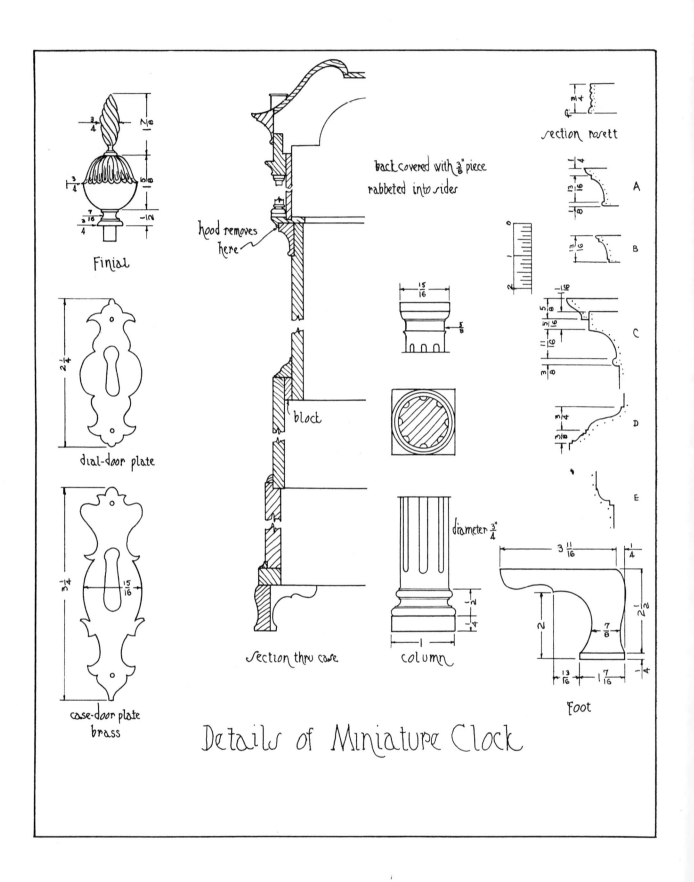

Finial

dial-door plate

case-door plate
brass

hood removes
here

block

Section thru case

back covered with ⅜" piece
rabbeted into sides

¹⁵⁄₁₆

⅝

column

diameter ¾"

section rosett

A

B

C

D

E

Foot

Details of Miniature Clock

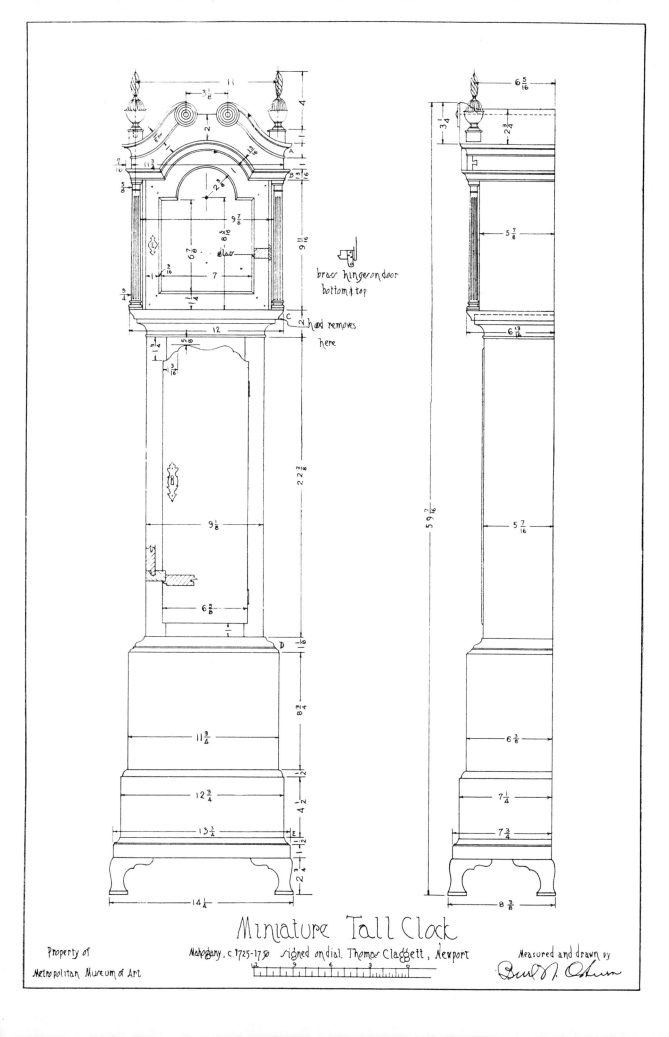

Miniature Tall Clock

Mahogany, c. 1725-1750   signed on dial, Thomas Claggett, Newport

Measured and drawn by

brass hinges on door
bottom & top

hood removes
here

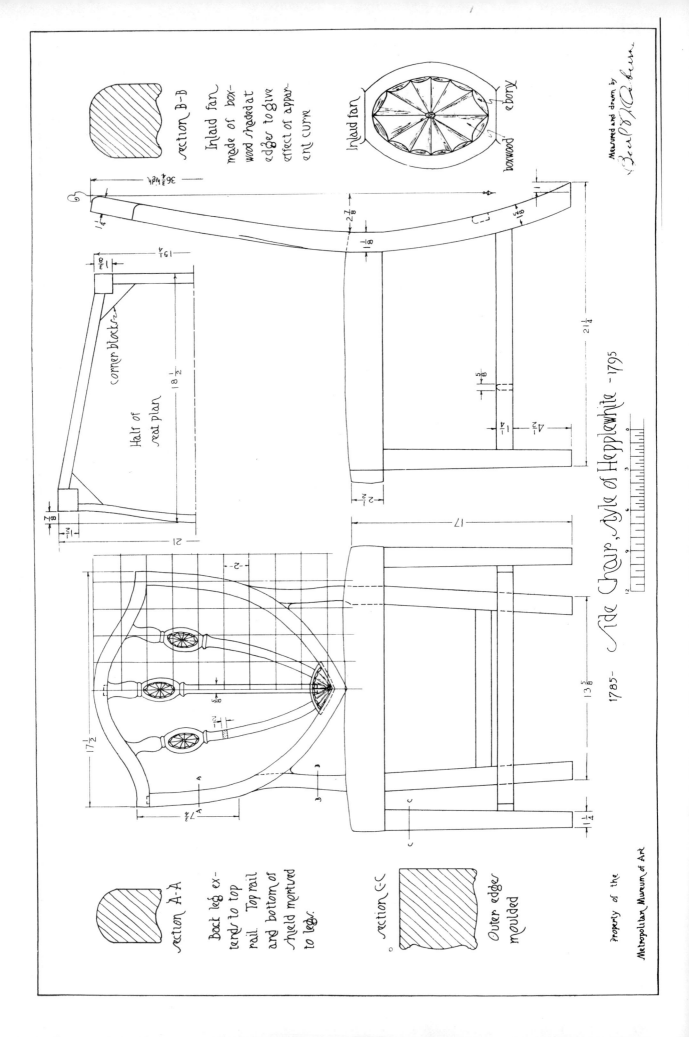

Section B-B

Inlaid fan made of boxwood shaded at edge to give effect of apparent curve

Inlaid fan

ebony

boxwood

Measured and drawn by
Bea P J Coburn

Section A-A

Back leg extend to top rail. Top rail and bottom of shield mortised to legs.

Section C-C

Outer edge moulded

corner blocks

Half of seat plan

1785 - Side Chair, Style of Hepplewhite - 1795

property of the
Metropolitan Museum of Art

SHIELD-BACK CHAIR

"In the year 1788 was published the "Cabinet-Maker's and Upholsterer's Guide." But notwithstanding the late date of Hepplewhite's book, if we compare some of the designs, particularly the chairs, we shall find that the work has already caught the decline, and perhaps in a little while will suddenly die in disorder."
—*The Cabinetmaker's and Upholsterer's Drawing Book, Thomas Sheraton, 1791*

This American-made chair, in the manner of Hepplewhite, is one that was termed by him a "Bannister-back" because of the curved splats. The back is the characteristic shield shape, the outline or frame of which is reeded on the front and rounded on the back. The front legs are tapered and are moulded on the front and outside surfaces. The back legs run through to the top rail, forming the sides of the shield above the seat. The top rail is mortised in three places on the under side for the splats, and near the ends to receive the tenons of the sides. The bottom of the shield is mortised to the back legs, and reeded continuously with the sides of the shield formed by the legs. The inlay in the splats is given the "fan" effect by heating the edges of the veneer in hot sand until it reaches the proper shade, though it is possible to buy these inlays made up.

Hepplewhite Shield-Back Chair

Note to Reprint Edition: This piece is no longer in the collection of the Metropolitan Museum of Art.

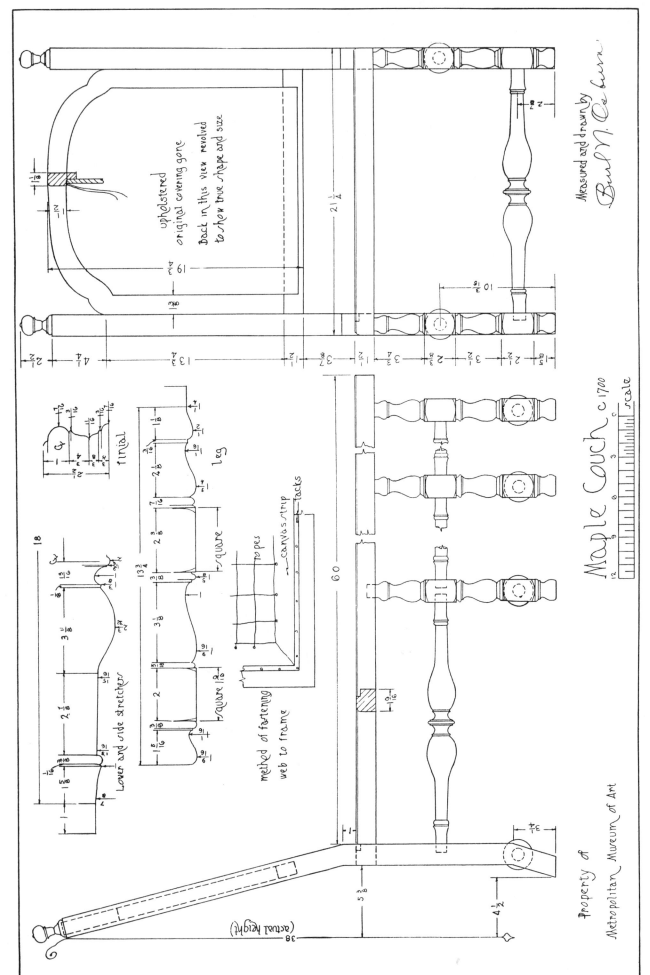

Maple Couch c.1700

Measured and drawn by
Burl N. Osburn

Property of
Metropolitan Museum of Art

upholstered original covering gone
Back in this view revolved to show true shape and size

finial

leg

Lower and side stretchers

method of fastening web to frame

ropes

canvas strip

tacks

square

scale

COUCH

"You cannot conceive how much we are distressed for wood. The poorer people go begging continually for every stick they use, and many of the better sort are under a necessity of keeping but one fire; some I know who have burnt chairs, hogsheads, barrels, chests of drawers, etc." —Chief Justice Sewell, 1780

The couch is similar in construction to a chair. The four lower rounds and six side stretchers are turned exactly alike. The back and three pairs of legs are assembled separately; then the side stretchers are connected. After this, the frame is bored to receive the legs, and the sides of the frame are joined to the straight legs with tenons. The inner edge of the frame is rabbeted deep enough to permit the strip of canvas to be tacked down, yet be lower than the top of the frame. Light ropes are run through the canvas at intervals of a few inches. The pad, or mattress, is laid on this net, and tied to the head piece and the legs.

The end view shows the back revolved to show its true size and shape, consequently the dimensions will not check with the height shown in the front view. The turned ornament on the back may be put on with a dowel, and the square part rounded off to it, though the original is turned directly on the leg. This turning is typical of the English Restoration furniture.

Couch—American—Seventeenth Century

Note to Reprint Edition: This piece is no longer in the collection of the Metropolitan Museum of Art.

DINING TABLE

*"I find cabinetmakers in employ all over this country, and it is an occupation which deserves encouragement * * I always judge the housewifery of the lady of the mansion by the appearance of the sideboard and tables."*
—*DeWitt Clinton, 1820*

This table shows some of the best characteristics of Phyfe furniture. Its construction is rather unusual, at least for modern work, in that the top tips to a vertical position if desired. When placed horizontally, a pair of locks, operated simultaneously by an iron pull, hold it in place. On top of the shaft is a horizontal cap, strengthened on the end grain by two battens. At one end of this cap, a curved vertical piece is securely fastened with dowels cut on each end. Battens, gained into the under side of the top, far enough apart to slip over the sides of the horizontal cap, swing on these dowels. The axis, or center of inclination, for locating the dowels on the base, and the holes in the battens, can be determined from the drawing. The legs are reeded on the upper side, and end in brass feet fitted with casters. They are fastened to the shaft by tenons. Sometimes, the straight, lower part of the shaft is made separate from the remainder, and the legs joined to it. An iron rod, with threads on the lower end, is run through the entire shaft, holding it together.

Duncan Phyfe Dining Table

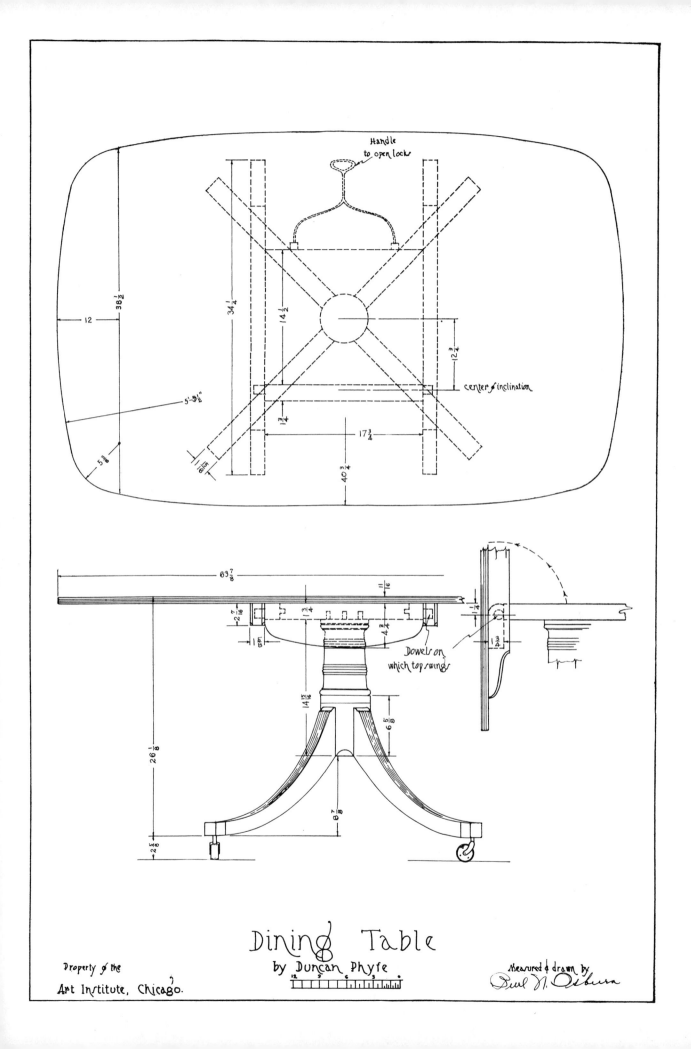

Handle
to open locks

center of inclination

Dowels on
which top swings

Dining Table
by Duncan Phyfe

Measured & drawn by
Paul N. Osburn

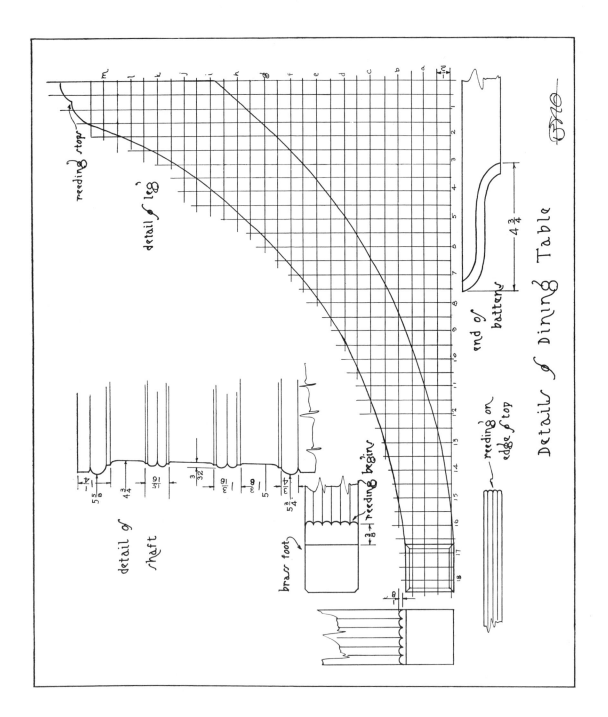

reeding stop

detail of leg

detail of shaft

reeding on edge of top

end of batten

4¾

reeding begin

brass foot

Details of Dining Table

CVO

HIGH-BOY

"Of the black walnut trees there is yet a sufficient quantity. However, careless people take pains enough to destroy them, and some peasants even use them for fewel."
                                                                    —extract, 1748

The high-boy originally helped to supply the storage space in the closet-less houses of the day. It was made in two sections, to be separated when moved. Occasionally, brass handles are found on the sides of the upper part, though probably mostly as a matter of decoration. This high-boy separates at the cove mould. The framework of the upper section is very simple; the drawer rails and runners show their construction on the front. The edges of the sides, rails, and top stile are reeded as shown in the detail.

The lower case sides and front apron are flush with the legs, and in the original are veneered. Each drawer fits between stiles about eight inches in depth, and rests on runners extending from the back to the front rails. These rails are reeded as on the upper section. The framework of rails and stiles is fastened to the ends and back, and rests on the front apron. Above the body of the lower part is a rounded frame on which the upper section rests. The juncture is covered with a cove.

The original is veneered with matched, figured walnut; the drawer edges are banded with darker grained wood. The brass work on this piece is not comparable to that of the later pieces.

Note to Reprint Edition: This piece is no longer in the collection of the Metropolitan Museum of Art.

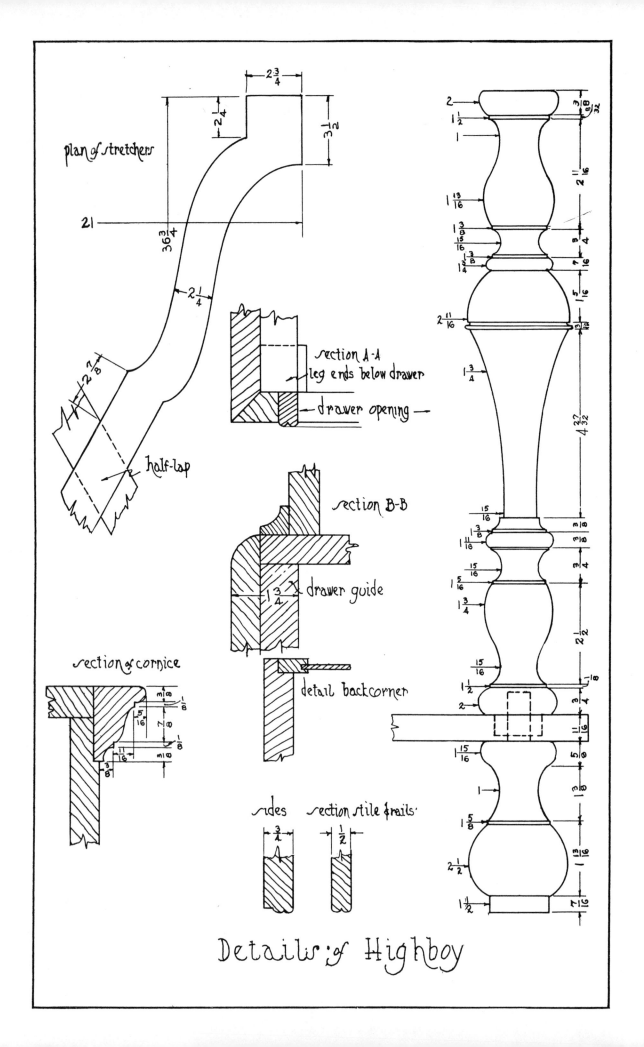

plan of stretchers

$2\frac{3}{4}$

$2\frac{1}{4}$

$3\frac{1}{2}$

21

$36\frac{3}{4}$

$2\frac{1}{4}$

$2\frac{7}{8}$

half-lap

section A-A
leg ends below drawer

— drawer opening —

section B-B

$1\frac{3}{4}$ drawer guide

detail back corner

section of cornice

$3\frac{1}{8}$
$1\frac{5}{16}$
$\frac{7}{8}$
$\frac{1}{8}$
$\frac{11}{16}$
$\frac{3}{8}$
$3\frac{1}{8}$

sides   section stile & rails

$\frac{3}{4}$ $\frac{1}{2}$

2
$1\frac{1}{2}$
1
$\frac{3}{8}$ $\frac{8}{32}$

$2\frac{11}{16}$

$1\frac{13}{16}$

$1\frac{3}{8}$
$1\frac{15}{16}$
$1\frac{3}{8}$
$1\frac{1}{4}$

$\frac{3}{4}$ $\frac{15}{16}$
$\frac{7}{16}$

$1\frac{5}{16}$

$2\frac{11}{16}$ $\frac{13}{16}$

$1\frac{3}{4}$

$4\frac{27}{32}$

$\frac{15}{16}$
$1\frac{3}{8}$
$1\frac{11}{16}$

$\frac{15}{16}$

$1\frac{1}{16}$

$1\frac{3}{4}$

$3\frac{1}{8}$
$3\frac{1}{8}$

$\frac{3}{4}$

$2\frac{1}{2}$

$\frac{15}{16}$

$1\frac{1}{2}$

2

$\frac{1}{8}$
$\frac{3}{4}$

$1\frac{1}{16}$

$\frac{15}{16}$

$\frac{5}{8}$

1

$1\frac{3}{8}$

$1\frac{5}{8}$

$2\frac{1}{2}$

$1\frac{13}{16}$

$1\frac{1}{2}$ $\frac{7}{16}$

Details of Highboy

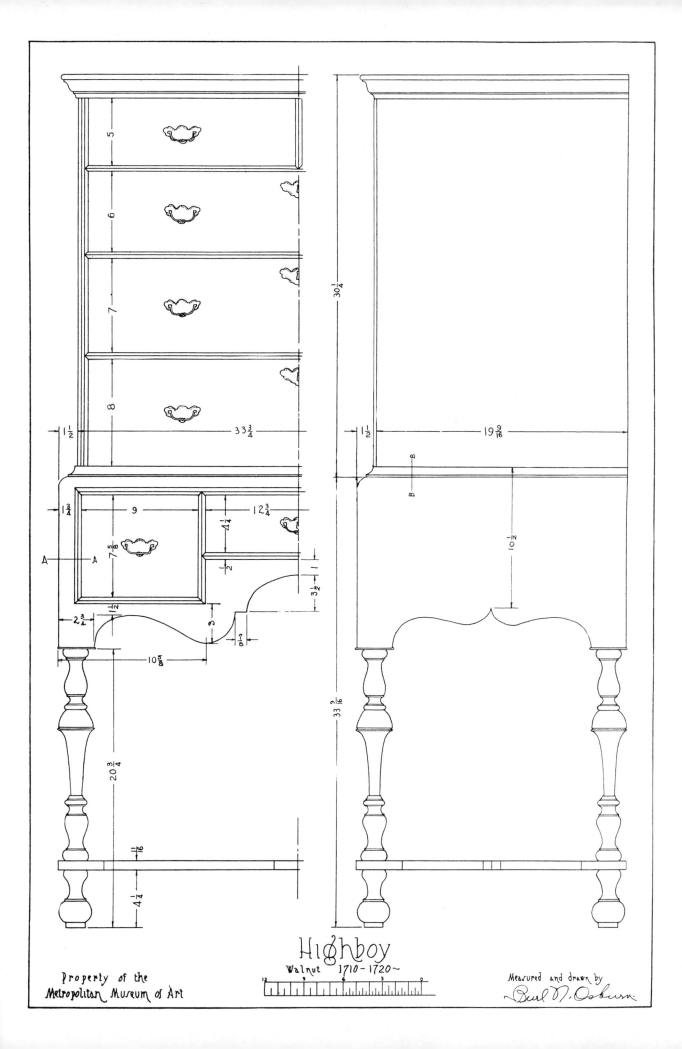

Highboy

Walnut 1710-1720~

Measured and drawn by

Paul N. Osburn

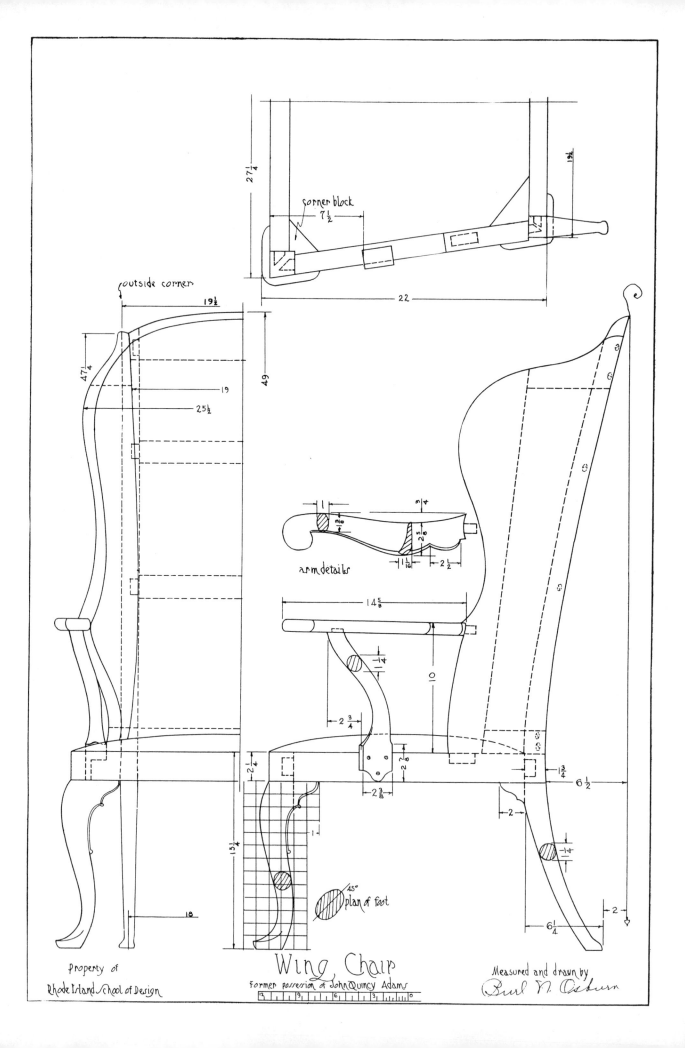

corner block

outside corner

arm details

plan of foot

45°

Wing Chair

Former possession of John Quincy Adams

Measured and drawn by

Burl N. Osburn

WING CHAIR

It was obviously impossible to secure the exact construction of this chair, so that that which is shown in the drawings is only a suggestion. The two front legs, back legs, arms, and arm supports are all of mahogany. The remainder should be of soft wood, since it holds the upholstery nails better than hard wood. The back is made as a frame, of which the back legs form a part. The braced frame of the seat is joined to the front and back legs as shown in the plan view. The two wings are constructed separately, and the arms and supports are joined to them. The wing framework should be made so that it is tenoned to the seat and back frame, but it is not to be glued. The back is first covered, and the finish cloth is applied only to the inside. The seat may be completely covered. The two wings are next finished in the same manner. They are then set in place on the chair, and the screws that hold it in place are put in. The back cloth is then run across the two wings and the back.

The front legs are made as those on the Essex Dresser or Four-Poster. The back legs are cut to their greatest thickness, and the exposed part is rounded with a spoke shave. The braces on these legs are made and applied the same way as those on the front.

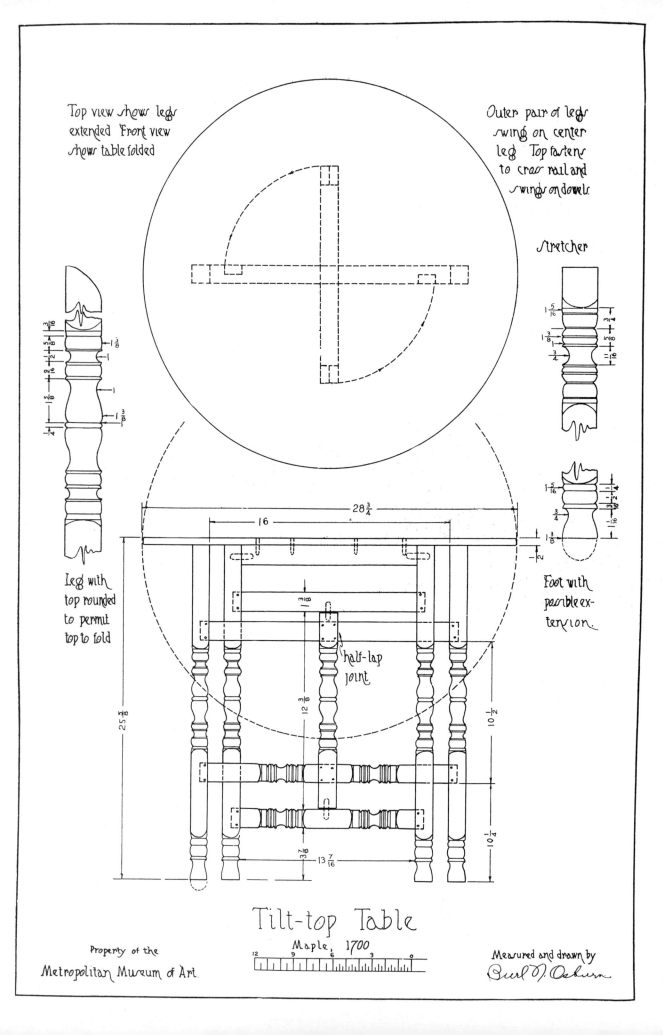

Top view shows legs extended Front view shows table folded

Outer pair of legs swing on center leg Top fastens to cross rail and swings on dowels.

Stretcher

Leg with top rounded to permit top to fold

half-lap joint

Foot with possible extension.

28¾

16

25⅝

12⅜

10½

10¼

3⅞

13⁷⁄₁₆

Tilt-top Table

Maple, 1700

Measured and drawn by
Burl N. Osburn

TILT-TOP TABLE

"i fire shovell and j pr. tongs wth copper topps
i boxe wth 8 fethers for ye bedds
i little square table of walnuttree
i folding table for the window."
                            —*Inventory of an English Hall, 1625*

This folding table is often called a "tuckaway" table. It is a type very popular and practical today. The top may be tilted to a vertical position when the legs are folded together, and so occupies a very small space. The outer pair of legs is joined by two cross stretchers to the center leg, which turns on dowels inserted in the two stretchers connecting the inner pair of legs. The top is joined by dowels run directly through the top to a cross-piece which fits between the inner pair of legs and turns on dowels inserted in them. The tops of all four legs are rounded, so that when the legs are folded together, all bevels will slant in the same direction. All tenons are pegged, or secured by small dowels run through the joint. The feet of the original were probably cut off short at some later date, to permit casters to be used.

The table is of maple that has developed a soft brown color, due to the oil and wax with which it was finished.

Tilt-Top Table

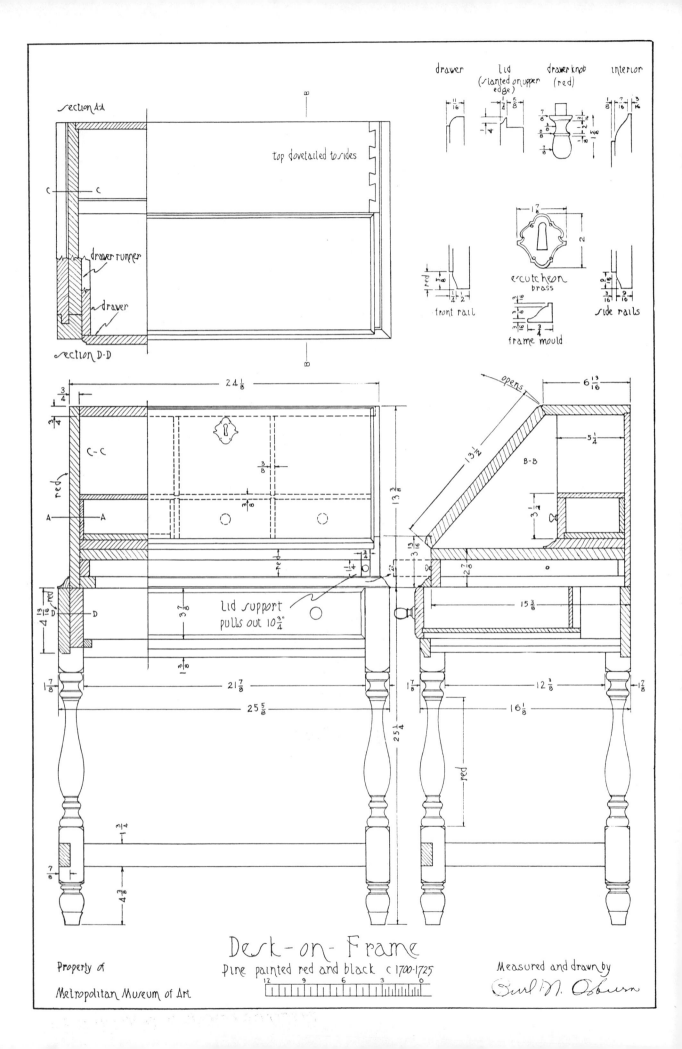

section A-A

drawer   lid   drawer knob   interior
(slanted on upper   (red)
edge)

top dovetailed to sides

c — c

drawer runner

drawer

section D-D

escutcheon
brass

front rail

frame mould

side rails

24 1/8

C-C

red

A — A

opens

6 13/16

5 1/4

B-B

3 1/2

13 1/2

13 3/8

D — D

4 13/16 red

lid support
pulls out 10 3/4"

3 7/8

3 7/8

2 7/8

15 3/8

1 7/8

21 7/8

25 5/8

25 1/4

1 7/8

12 3/8

1 7/8

16 1/8

red

3/4

7/8

4 3/8

Desk-on-Frame
Pine painted red and black c 1700-1725

12 9 6 3 0

Measured and drawn by

Carl M. Osburn

DESK-ON-FRAME

"All Boston was in confusion, (at the threatened invasion) packing up and carting out of town household furniture, military stores, etc. Not less than a thousand teams were employed on Friday and Saturday; and to their shame be it told, not a small trunk would they carry under eight dollars."
—*Abigale Adams to John Adams, 1775*

The small desk boxes, sometimes used to hold the family bible, or in other instances, writing materials, were originally flat-topped. They were soon given a slanting top to facilitate writing. Then they were placed on frames, some of them with one or two drawers in the frame. The construction of this piece shows that the two parts were not yet thoroughly amalgamated into the slant-top desk of later days. The writing leaf rests on two draw supports, pulled out for this purpose from under the desk. These should fit so as to move easily, yet when pulled out, they should not incline downward. A dowel is put in the inner side at a point to strike the front rail of the desk. This will regulate the distance the slide may be drawn. The drawers in the desk are dovetailed, front and back, and in the case of the three small drawers, the bottom is set at the bottom of the sides. The top is dovetailed to the sides so that the joints show on top. The front edge of the top is beveled to permit the slightly-beveled lid to drop into place.

The desk rests on strips fastened to the inner side of the side and back rails of the frame. The frame and desk are joined and held by the moulded piece that runs around three sides. The legs are mortised to rails and to the stretchers that continue around the four sides, flush with the outside of the square part of the leg.

The original desk is painted a dead black and a dull brick red.

Note to Reprint Edition: This piece is no longer in the collection of the Metropolitan Museum of Art.

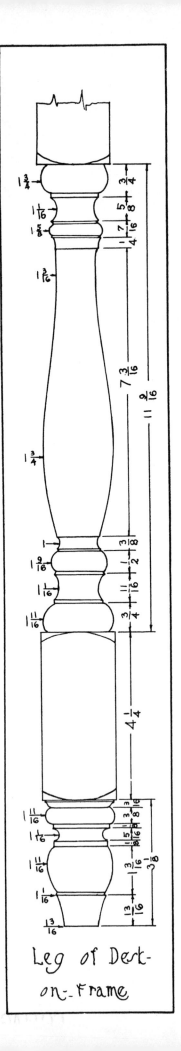

$1\frac{3}{4}$

$1\frac{1}{16}$

$1\frac{5}{8}$

$1\frac{3}{16}$

$\frac{3}{4}$

$\frac{5}{8}$

$\frac{7}{16}$

$4\frac{1}{4}$

$7\frac{3}{16}$

$11\frac{9}{16}$

$1\frac{3}{4}$

1

$1\frac{9}{16}$

$1\frac{1}{16}$

$1\frac{11}{16}$

$\frac{3}{8}$

$\frac{1}{2}$

$\frac{11}{16}$

$\frac{3}{4}$

$4\frac{1}{4}$

$1\frac{11}{16}$

$1\frac{1}{8}$

$1\frac{11}{16}$

$1\frac{1}{16}$

$1\frac{3}{16}$

$\frac{3}{8}$

$\frac{5}{8}$

$\frac{3}{16}$

$\frac{3}{16}$

$3\frac{1}{8}$

$\frac{13}{16}$

Leg of Desk-
on-Frame

Dover Books on Art

MASTERPIECES OF FURNITURE, Verna Cook Salomonsky.
Photographs and measured drawings of some of the finest examples of Colonial American, 17th century English, Windsor, Sheraton, Hepplewhite, Chippendale, Louis XIV, Queen Anne, and various other furniture styles. The textual matter includes information on traditions, characteristics, background, etc. of various pieces. 101 plates. Bibliography. 224pp. 7⅞ x 10¾.
21381-1 Paperbound $4.50

PRIMITIVE ART, Franz Boas. In this exhaustive volume, a great American anthropologist analyzes all the fundamental traits of primitive art, covering the formal element in art, representative art, symbolism, style, literature, music, and the dance. Illustrations of Indian embroidery, paleolithic paintings, woven blankets, wing and tail designs, totem poles, cutlery, earthenware, baskets and many other primitive objects and motifs. Over 900 illustrations. 376pp. 5⅜ x 8.   20025-6 Paperbound $3.75

AN INTRODUCTION TO A HISTORY OF WOODCUT, A. M. Hind. Nearly all of this authoritative 2-volume set is devoted to the 15th century—the period during which the woodcut came of age as an important art form. It is the most complete compendium of information on this period, the artists who contributed to it, and their technical and artistic accomplishments. Profusely illustrated with cuts by 15th century masters, and later works for comparative purposes. 484 illustrations. 5 indexes. Total of xi + 838pp. 5⅜ x 8½. Two-vols. 20952-0,20953-0 Paperbound $10.50

A HISTORY OF ENGRAVING AND ETCHING, A. M. Hind. Beginning with the anonymous masters of 15th century engraving, this highly regarded and thorough survey carries you through Italy, Holland, and Germany to the great engravers and beginnings of etching in the 16th century, through the portrait engravers, master etchers, practicioners of mezzotint, crayon manner and stipple, aquatint, color prints, to modern etching in the period just prior to World War I. Beautifully illustrated—sharp clear prints on heavy opaque paper. Author's preface. 3 appendixes. 111 illustrations. xviii + 487 pp. 5⅜ x 8½.
20954-7 Paperbound $5.00

ART STUDENTS' ANATOMY, E. J. Farris. Teaching anatomy by using chiefly living objects for illustration, this study has enjoyed long popularity and success in art courses and home-study programs. All the basic elements of the human anatomy are illustrated in minute detail, diagrammed and pictured as they pass through common movements and actions. 158 drawings, photographs, and roentgenograms. Glossary of anatomical terms. x + 159pp. 5⅝ x 8⅜.   20744-7 Paperbound $2.50

COLONIAL LIGHTING, A. H. Hayward. The only book to cover the fascinating story of lamps and other lighting devices in America. Beginning with rush light holders used by the early settlers, it ranges through the elaborate chandeliers of the Federal period, illustrating 647 lamps. Of great value to antique collectors, designers, and historians of arts and crafts. Revised and enlarged by James R. Marsh. xxxi + 198pp. 5⅝ x 8¼.
20975-X Paperbound $3.50

Dover Books on Art

200 DECORATIVE TITLE-PAGES, edited by A. Nesbitt. Fascinating and informative from a historical point of view, this beautiful collection of decorated titles will be a great inspiration to students of design, commercial artists, advertising designers, etc. A complete survey of the genre from the first known decorated title to work in the first decades of this century. Bibliography and sources of the plates. 222pp. 8⅜ x 11¼.

21264-5 Paperbound $5.00

ON THE LAWS OF JAPANESE PAINTING, H. P. Bowie. This classic work on the philosophy and technique of Japanese art is based on the author's first-hand experiences studying art in Japan. Every aspect of Japanese painting is described: the use of the brush and other materials; laws governing conception and execution; subjects for Japanese paintings, etc. The best possible substitute for a series of lessons from a great Oriental master. Index. xv + 117pp. + 66 plates. 6⅛ x 9¼.

20030-2 Paperbound $4.50

A HANDBOOK•OF ANATOMY FOR ART STUDENTS, Arthur Thomson. This long-popular text teaches any student, regardless of level of technical competence, all the subtleties of human anatomy. Clear photographs, numerous line sketches and diagrams of bones, joints, etc. Use it as a text for home study, as a supplement to life class work, or as a lifelong sourcebook and reference volume. Author's prefaces. 67 plates, containing 40 line drawings, 86 photographs—mostly full page. 211 figures. Appendix. Index. xx + 459pp. 5⅜ x 8⅜. 21163-0 Paperbound $5.00

WHITTLING AND WOODCARVING, E. J. Tangerman. With this book, a beginner who is moderately handy can whittle or carve scores of useful objects, toys for children, gifts, or simply pass hours creatively and enjoyably. "Easy as well as instructive reading," N. Y. Herald Tribune Books. 464 illustrations, with appendix and index. x + 293pp. 5½ x 8⅛.

20965-2 Paperbound $2.75

ONE HUNDRED AND ONE PATCHWORK PATTERNS, Ruby Short McKim. Whether you have made a hundred quilts or none at all, you will find this the single most useful book on quiltmaking. There are 101 full patterns (all exact size) with full instructions for cutting and sewing. In addition there is some really choice folklore about the origin of the ingenious pattern names: "Monkey Wrench," "Road to California," "Drunkard's Path," "Crossed Canoes," to name a few. Over 500 illustrations. 124 pp. 7⅞ x 10¾. 20773-0 Paperbound $2.50

ART AND GEOMETRY, W. M. Ivins, Jr. Challenges the idea that the foundations of modern thought were laid in ancient Greece. Pitting Greek tactile-muscular intuitions of space against modern visual intuitions, the author, for 30 years curator of prints, Metropolitan Museum of Art, analyzes the differences between ancient and Renaissance painting and sculpture and tells of the first fruitful investigations of perspective. x + 113pp. 5⅜ x 8⅜. 20941-5 Paperbound $2.00

PRINCIPLES OF ART HISTORY, H. Wölfflin. This remarkably instructive work demonstrates the tremendous change in artistic conception from the 14th to the 18th centuries, by analyzing 164 works by Botticelli, Dürer, Hobbema, Holbein, Hals, Titian, Rembrandt, Vermeer, etc., and pointing out exactly what is meant by "baroque," "classic," "primitive," "picturesque," and other basic terms of art history and criticism. "A remarkable lesson in the art of seeing," SAT. REV. OF LITERATURE. Translated from the 7th German edition. 150 illus. 254pp. 6⅛ x 9¼.   20276-3 Paperbound $3.50

FOUNDATIONS OF MODERN ART, A. Ozenfant. Stimulating discussion of human creativity from paleolithic cave painting to modern painting, architecture, decorative arts. Fully illustrated with works of Gris, Lipchitz, Léger, Picasso, primitive, modern artifacts, architecture, industrial art, much more. 226 illustrations. 368pp. 6⅛ x 9¼.   20215-1 Paperbound $5.00

METALWORK AND ENAMELLING, H. Maryon. Probably the best book ever written on the subject. Tells everything necessary for the home manufacture of jewelry, rings, ear pendants, bowls, etc. Covers materials, tools, soldering, filigree, setting stones, raising patterns, repoussé work, damascening, niello, cloisonné, polishing, assaying, casting, and dozens of other techniques. The best substitute for apprenticeship to a master metalworker. 363 photos and figures. 374pp. 5½ x 8½.
22702-2 Paperbound $3.50

SHAKER FURNITURE, E. D. and *F. Andrews.* The most illuminating study of Shaker furniture ever written. Covers chronology, craftsmanship, houses, shops, etc. Includes over 200 photographs of chairs, tables, clocks, beds, benches, etc. "Mr. & Mrs. Andrews know all there is to know about Shaker furniture," Mark Van Doren, NATION. 48 full-page plates. 192pp. 7⅞ x 10¾.   20679-3 Paperbound $4.00

LETTERING AND ALPHABETS, J. A. Cavanagh. An unabridged reissue of "Lettering," containing the full discussion, analysis, illustration of 89 basic hand lettering styles based on Caslon, Bodoni, Gothic, many other types. Hundreds of technical hints on construction, strokes, pens, brushes, etc. 89 alphabets, 72 lettered specimens, which may be reproduced permission-free. 121pp. 9¾ x 8.   20053-1 Paperbound $2.50

THE HUMAN FIGURE IN MOTION, Eadweard Muybridge. The largest collection in print of Muybridge's famous high-speed action photos. 4789 photographs in more than 500 action-strip-sequences (at shutter speeds up to 1/6000th of a second) illustrate men, women, children—mostly undraped—performing such actions as walking, running, getting up, lying down, carrying objects, throwing, etc. "An unparalleled dictionary of action for all artists," AMERICAN ARTIST. 390 full-page plates, with 4789 photographs. Heavy glossy stock, reinforced binding with headbands. 7⅞ x 10¾.   20204-6 Clothbound $12.50

ART ANATOMY, Dr. William Rimmer. One of the few books on art anatomy that are themselves works of art, this is a faithful reproduction (rearranged for handy use) of the extremely rare masterpiece of the famous 19th century anatomist, sculptor, and art teacher. Beautiful, clear line drawings show every part of the body—bony structure, muscles, features, etc. Unusual are the sections on falling bodies, foreshortenings, muscles in tension, grotesque personalities, and Rimmer's remarkable interpretation of emotions and personalities as expressed by facial features. It will supplement every other book on art anatomy you are likely to have. Reproduced clearer than the lithographic original (which sells for $500 on up on the rare book market.) Over 1,200 illustrations. xiii + 153pp. 7¾ x 10¾.

20908-3 Paperbound $3.75

THE CRAFTSMAN'S HANDBOOK, Cennino Cennini. The finest English translation of IL LIBRO DELL' ARTE, the 15th century introduction to art technique that is both a mirror of Quatrocento life and a source of many useful but nearly forgotten facets of the painter's art. 4 illustrations. xxvii + 142pp. D. V. Thompson, translator. 5⅜ x 8.

20054-X Paperbound $2.50

THE BROWN DECADES, Lewis Mumford. A picture of the "buried renaissance" of the post-Civil War period, and the founding of modern architecture (Sullivan, Richardson, Root, Roebling), landscape development (Marsh, Olmstead, Eliot), and the graphic arts (Homer, Eakins, Ryder). 2nd revised, enlarged edition. Bibliography. 12 illustrations. xiv + 266 pp. 5⅜ x 8.

20200-3 Paperbound $2.00

THE STYLES OF ORNAMENT, A. Speltz. The largest collection of line ornament in print, with 3750 numbered illustrations arranged chronologically from Egypt, Assyria, Greeks, Romans, Etruscans, through Medieval, Renaissance, 18th century, and Victorian. No permissions, no fees needed to use or reproduce illustrations. 400 plates with 3750 illustrations. Bibliography. Index. 640pp. 6 x 9.

20577-6 Paperbound $5.50

THE ART OF ETCHING, E. S. Lumsden. Every step of the etching process from essential materials to completed proof is carefully and clearly explained, with 24 annotated plates exemplifying every technique and approach discussed. The book also features a rich survey of the art, with 105 annotated plates by masters. Invaluable for beginner to advanced etcher. 374pp. 5⅜ x 8.

20049-3 Paperbound $3.75

OF THE JUST SHAPING OF LETTERS, Albrecht Dürer. This remarkable volume reveals Albrecht Dürer's rules for the geometric construction of Roman capitals and the formation of Gothic lower case and capital letters, complete with construction diagrams and directions. Of considerable practical interest to the contemporary illustrator, artist, and designer. Translated from the Latin text of the edition of 1535 by R. T. Nichol. Numerous letterform designs, construction diagrams, illustrations. iv + 43pp. 7⅞ x 10¾.

21306-4 Paperbound $2.00

PINE FURNITURE OF EARLY NEW ENGLAND, R. H. Kettell. Over 400 illustrations, over 50 working drawings of early New England chairs, benches, beds, cupboards, mirrors, shelves, tables, other furniture esteemed for simple beauty and character. "Rich store of illustrations . . . emphasizes the individuality and varied design," ANTIQUES. 413 illustrations, 55 working drawings. 475pp. 8 x 10¾.   20145-7 Clothbound $12.50

BASIC BOOKBINDING, A. W. Lewis. Enables both beginners and experts to rebind old books or bind paperbacks in hard covers. Treats materials, tools; gives step-by-step instruction in how to collate a book, sew it, back it, make boards, etc. 261 illus. Appendices. 155pp. 5⅜ x 8.   20169-4 Paperbound $1.75

DESIGN MOTIFS OF ANCIENT MEXICO, J. Enciso. Nearly 90% of these 766 superb designs from Aztec, Olmec, Totonac, Maya, and Toltec origins are unobtainable elsewhere. Contains plumed serpents, wind gods, animals, demons, dancers, monsters, etc. Excellent applied design source. Originally $17.50. 766 illustrations, thousands of motifs. 192pp. 6⅛ x 9¼.
                                        20084-1 Paperbound $2.50

A DIDEROT PICTORIAL ENCYCLOPEDIA OF TRADES AND INDUSTRY. Manufacturing and the Technical Arts in Plates Selected from "L'Encyclopédie ou Dictionnaire Raisonné des Sciences, des Arts, et des Métiers," of Denis Diderot, edited with text by C. Gillispie. Over 2000 illustrations on 485 full-page plates. Magnificent 18th-century engravings of men, women, and children working at such trades as milling flour, cheesemaking, charcoal burning, mining, silverplating, shoeing horses, making fine glass, printing, hundreds more, showing details of machinery, different steps in sequence, etc. A remarkable art work, but also the largest collection of working figures in print, copyright-free, for art directors, designers, etc. Two vols. 920pp. 9 x 12. Heavy library cloth.   22284-5, 22283-3 Two volume set $30.00

SILK SCREEN TECHNIQUES, J. Biegeleisen, M. Cohn. A practical step-by-step home course in one of the most versatile, least expensive graphic arts processes. How to build an inexpensive silk screen, prepare stencils, print, achieve special textures, use color, etc. Every step explained, diagrammed. 149 illustrations, 201pp. 6⅛ x 9¼.   20433-2 Paperbound $2.50

STICKS AND STONES, Lewis Mumford. An examination of forces influencing American architecture: the medieval tradition in early New England, the classical influence in Jefferson's time, the Brown Decades, the imperial facade, the machine age, etc. "A truly remarkable book," SAT. REV. OF LITERATURE. 2nd revised edition. 21 illus. xvii + 240pp. 5⅜ x 8.
                                        20202-X Paperbound $2.50

THE AUTOBIOGRAPHY OF AN IDEA, Louis Sullivan. The architect whom Frank Lloyd Wright called "the master," records the development of the theories that revolutionized America's skyline. 34 full-page plates of Sullivan's finest work. New introduction by R. M. Line. xiv + 335pp. 5⅜ x 8.
                                        20281-X Paperbound $3.50

DESIGN AND FIGURE CARVING, E. J. Tangerman. "Anyone who can peel a potato can carve," states the author, and in this unusual book he shows you how, covering every stage in detail from very simple exercises working up to museum-quality pieces. Terrific aid for hobbyists, arts and crafts counselors, teachers, those who wish to make reproductions for the commercial market. Appendix: How to Enlarge a Design. Brief bibliography. Index. 1298 figures. x + 289pp. 5⅜ x 8½.

21209-2 Paperbound $3.00

THE STANDARD BOOK OF QUILT MAKING AND COLLECTING, M. Ickis. Even if you are a beginner, you will soon find yourself quilting like an expert, by following these clearly drawn patterns, photographs, and step-by-step instructions. Learn how to plan the quilt, to select the pattern to harmonize with the design and color of the room, to choose materials. Over 40 full-size patterns. Index. 483 illustrations. One color plate. xi + 276pp. 6¾ x 9½.

20582-7 Paperbound **$3.50**

A HISTORY OF COSTUME, Carl Köhler. The most reliable and authentic account of the development of dress from ancient times through the 19th century. Based on actual pieces of clothing that have survived, using paintings, statues and other reproductions only where originals no longer exist. Hundreds of illustrations, including detailed patterns for many articles. Highly useful for theatre and movie directors, fashion designers, illustrators, teachers. Edited and augmented by Emma von Sichart. Translated by Alexander K. Dallas. 594 illustrations. 464pp. 5⅛ x 7⅛.

21030-8 Paperbound $4.00

Dover publishes books on commercial art, art history, crafts, design, ar/ classics; also books on music, literature, science, mathematics, puzzles and entertainments, chess, engineering, biology, philosophy, psychology, languages, history, and other fields. For free circulars write to Dept. DA, Dover Publications, Inc., 180 Varick St., New York, N.Y. 10014.